DAILY J

alone with GOD

jason janz

Greenville, South Carolina

Alone with God Daily Journal

Jason Janz

Design by Craig Oesterling
Composition by Melissa Matos

Greenville, SC 29614

Printed in the United States of America

ISBN 1-59166-676-7

15 14 13 12 11 10 9 8 7 6 5 4 3 2 1

Introduction

This journal is a companion to the book, *Alone with God*. The book maps out an eight-step plan for having dynamic daily devotions. One of the keys to having quality time alone with God is planning your devotions before you begin them. I would like to encourage you to plan your time with God just like you plan everything else in your life. I recommend your taking five minutes to plan before you do anything. To follow the plan, I have created two pages to help you have a refreshing daily quiet time. The first page is the *Alone with God* Devotional Planner. The second page is the *Alone with God* Devotional Journal. Before you begin your quiet time, fill out each of the "My Plan Today" sections of the Devotional Planner. The entire plan is comprised of eight steps. Below are the eight steps.

1. Preparation Step

This step involves preparing your heart to worship God through prayer, song, or the reading of a few pages from a Christian book. This is the time you spend warming up your spiritual muscles. Do not start your devotions by whipping out your Bible and reading. Take time to prepare your heart. During this time it is important to declare your intention to obey God no matter what He may tell you.

2. Confession Step

The Bible says in 1 John 1:9, "If we confess our sins, he is faithful and just to forgive us our sins and to cleanse us from all unrighteousness." The Greek word

confess is *homologeo* which means "to say the same thing." Confession simply means to agree with God about sin. I simply say to God, "God, I agree with you that what I thought yesterday was evil and against You. I agree that the anger that I let fester in my spirit was wrong. It was sin." I do not need to spend hours in weeping or self-torment. God wants me to simply recognize and grasp the fact that I missed the mark in my life. On your daily Devotional Planner page, I have put the words "Search Me, O God" into the regular planning space. I did this because nobody wants to write out their sins in a journal. However this should be a daily reminder for you for God to search your heart.

3. Revelation Step

The Revelation Step involves reading one passage of the Bible with the purpose of learning about God—His revelation to you. The first step in this phase is to pick a book of the Bible to study and then to move systematically through this book, journaling your thoughts about God. During this step, you are endeavoring to find God in the passage. As you are reading, ask yourself the question, "What is God trying to show me about Himself?" You are endeavoring to learn more about God. I started out *Alone with God* by studying the book of Acts. Each day I picked the next chapter and began to chronicle what I learned.

I divided the Bible into three sections in the appendix (see p. A5) for you: Easy, Moderate, and Difficult. Those categories will help you choose a book appropriate to the level of difficulty you desire at this stage of your spiritual life. If you have not had a regular devotional time with God, I suggest you start with the easy books. If you have never read the Bible systematically, I have marked the books that would be best for you to begin with. However, if you are a lifelong Bible student, I suggest the difficult books. After you complete one book, choose another one and continue to learn and journal about your great God. If you would like some Bible helps to aid your understanding, I recommend the use of some Bible commentaries or a good study Bible.

4. Adoration Step

The Adoration Step involves prayer and songs of praise and thanksgiving to God. Praise is recognizing God for Who He is. How does someone praise God? I traveled in evangelism with an evangelist named Steve Pettit. He talks in a booklet he wrote about using the names of God to praise Him. (see appendix, pp. A6–10) He says, "Often when I am discouraged and my cup is empty, I praise God for Who He is, and I say, 'Jehovah-Shammah-the Lord our presence. Oh Lord, I need your presence. You are Jehovah-Shammah. You are my God. You are here. You will never leave me nor forsake me. The Lord is with thee always, even unto the end of the world. Amen.' Before ten minutes have passed, I sense the wonderful presence of the Lord."[1]

Thanksgiving is thanking God for what He has done. Thanksgiving is also a regular theme throughout Scripture. Thanksgiving is offered for everything including:

- *Deliverance from affliction (Jonah 2:9)*
- *God's provision (2 Corinthians 9:11)*
- *Food (1 Timothy 4:3)*
- *Deliverance from enemies (2 Samuel 22:50)*
- *God's goodness (1 Chronicles 16:34)*
- *God's mercy (1 Chronicles. 16:41)*
- *God's holiness (Psalm 30:4)*
- *God's works (Psalm 105:1)*
- *Wisdom (Daniel 2:23)*
- *Answered prayer (John 11:41)*
- *Other believers (Romans 1:8, Philippians 1:3, 2 Thessalonians 1:3)*

This is a perfect place to interject music into your devotions. There are countless songs of praise to God to listen to, sing, or meditate on. I have included a section in the appendix (see pp. A1–2) for you to create a song index of Praise and Thanksgiving songs. If you do not know many songs, contact the music leader at your church to help you. A good songbook usually has an index where the songs are sorted topically. This can be a great help.

5. Transformation Step

The Transformation Step involves a responsive reading and prayer of one passage from Psalms or Proverbs. The emphasis is placed on praying the Scriptures to the Lord. You will take a passage of Scripture, read it, and then pray it back to God. By praying God's Word, you are letting His very thoughts penetrate your heart and mind.

---

[1] Pettit, Steve. *How to Pray Thirty Minutes a Day* (Pembine, WI: Heart Publications, 1996), 10–11.

For an example of a responsive reading, let's take Psalm 34:1–2. The passage reads:

"I will bless the Lord at all times: his praise shall continually be in my mouth. My soul shall make her boast in the Lord: the humble shall hear thereof, and be glad."

My Transformation Step reading is a prayer that could look like this:

Reading: *"I will bless the Lord at all times:"*

Response: *"God, I want to bless you this morning. You are my praise. I want to praise you all day, at all times."*

Reading: *"his praise shall continually be in my mouth."*

Response: *"God, may I praise you continually, to my family, to the people I work with, to those I talk with today."*

Reading: *"My soul shall make her boast in the Lord: the humble shall hear thereof, and be glad."*

Response: *"God, I not only want to praise you, I want to boast in you. I am proud to be able to call you my Lord. I do not want to be ashamed to speak of you always."*

6. Communication Step

This step involves personal prayer. Consider structuring your requests into the following categories:

- *Communicate with God about your personal needs. These are usually the things that come to your mind regarding your daily necessities.*
- *Communicate with God about the needs of others. Pray for those you know who need God's working in their lives.*
- *Communicate with God by casting your burdens and cares on Him. The Bible tells us to cast our cares upon God because He cares for us.*
- *Communicate with God by claiming His promises. Find a need that you have and a Bible promise that speaks to that need and claim it.*

7. Meditation Step

You have now reached the part of your quiet time where you will write. Steps seven and eight are on your Devotional Journal page. The first section of your journal is your Meditation Step. Now the goal is to write down what you have learned in the Word through your two reading times—the Revelation Step and the Transformation Step.

The greatest focus of meditation in the world is God. From your two readings, write out on your Devotional Journal page how God's character was revealed to you. Your first part of the journal will be a section for you to record what God showed you about Himself. Start by asking yourself, "What did I see about God today in His Word? What was He showing me about Himself?" Write it down. Try to keep a God-centered focus in your journaling. Keep in mind that the part of His glory He showed you is probably directly related to what He wants to work on in your life.

Meditation

What did God show me about Himself?

God is compassionate. At a tough time, Christ still healed the sick. He was selfless.

God is the great provider. He was not limited by lack of supply.

Now, look over the two passages you have read and locate one truth, verse, or thought to think on throughout the day. Find the core truth and write it out fully in the journal here:

What verse or truth from my two Bible readings will I meditate on day and night?

Psalm 34:4 I sought the Lord, and he heard me, and delivered me from all my fears.

There may be some days when no verse really jumps off the page at you. Some have advocated continued reading until you find something to meditate on. However, we all have a down day now and then. If you are just not "into it," you may be reading for a long time. Simply go to the appendix (see pp. A11–17) and pick a promise from the 100 Favorite Bible Promises list. Use one of these as your meditation truth for the day. And there is nothing wrong with picking a verse from previous days to meditate on.

Next you will want to find some way to keep that verse before you all day long. This truth needs to find its way into your heart so that you can personalize it to keep yourself from sinning against God (Psalm 119:11). You need to come up with a Meditation Reminder. This could mean writing it down on a 3X5 card or putting it into your daily planner so that you regularly see this divine truth throughout the day.

8. Application Step

The final step of *Alone with God* is to write down what God has told you to do. This is a crucial step because now you get a chance to take action. The Application Step is the crucial link between learning Who God is and changing to be more like Him. The Bible is very clear that we not only need to hear the Word, but do it (James 1:22). Chances are the Holy Spirit has brought some action steps to your mind. We can respond one of two ways to the Holy Spirit: obey the Spirit or quench the Spirit. Every time we refuse to obey His prompting, it is as though we are throwing cold water on the embers of a hot relationship with God. However, when you obey, you are enacting the blessings of God upon your life (John 14:21). The Holy Spirit may have prompted you to forgive someone, do a kind deed, become involved in a ministry, or work on your anger problem. Whatever He says, do it. I always get a kick out of the bumper sticker that reads, "Practice senseless acts of beauty and random acts of kindness." The good news about the Holy Spirit living inside me is that I do not have to do anything random or senseless. I can practice sensible acts of beauty and specific acts of kindness. Whatever the prompting may entail, it is important to write it down.

Application

What did God, through His Word, tell me to do?

I must realize that if God can walk on water and feed thousands with a small lunch, He can provide for my financial needs.
I need to selflessly serve my family by spending more time with my kids.
I must pray more! I must seek the Lord.

The last section of the journal page is entitled, "Other Thoughts." This is just space for you to write out your thoughts as it pertains to life!

The first six steps are on the *Alone with God* Devotional Planner page and the last two steps are on the *Alone with God* Devotional Journal page. Before you begin your quiet time, plan your devotions by filling out the My Plan Today sections of the Devotional Planner page. (See sample on next page)

This planning time should take no longer than five minutes, and the more you do it, the faster you will get at it. I encourage you to use variety and not to copy the previous day's plan. Once you are finished filling out the My Plan Today sections of the Devotional Planner, you are ready to begin your quiet time. The Devotional Journal page will be filled in at the conclusion of your quiet time.

Devotional Planner

Date: Sample Page

Preparation

Prayer ◆ Song ◆ Reading of a Christian book

My Plan Today:

Pray, sing "How Great Thou Art," read January 12 in Charles Spurgeon's **Morning and Evening** *devotional*

Confession

- Confession of known sin

My Plan Today:

Search Me, O God

Revelation

- Reading to know God through one Bible passage

My Plan Today:

Matthew 14

Adoration

- Prayer and songs of praise
- Prayer and songs of thanksgiving
- Praying the names of God

My Plan Today:

1. *Praise Him for what I learned in my Revelation step.*
2. *Pray names of God 1-2 (see appendix, pp. A6–10)*
3. *Prayer of thanksgiving for provision*
4. *Sing "Amazing Grace" and thank God for His great salvation*

Transformation

- Interactive reading and prayer of one chapter from Psalms or Proverbs

My Plan Today:

Psalm 34

Communication

- Prayer for personal needs
- Prayer for needs of others
- Prayer of casting cares upon the Lord
- Prayer of claiming a promise from God

My Plan Today:

Personal—bills, Mom's health, Every-Day list

Others—Monday list

Care-casting—future job decision

Promise—James 1:5

Time Schedule

Time Schedules

The actual time you spend will be approximately twenty or thirty minutes, divided into eight segments. I have mapped out below how I divide the time for either plan.

30-Minute Plan

1. Preparation-2 minutes
2. Confession-1 minute
3. Revelation-10 minutes
4. Adoration-4 minutes
5. Transformation-4 minutes
6. Communication-4 minutes

7. & 8. Meditation and Application 5 minutes

20-Minute Plan

1. Preparation-1 minute
2. Confession-1 minute
3. Revelation-8 minutes
4. Adoration-2 minutes
5. Transformation-3 minutes
6. Communication-3 minutes

7. & 8. Meditation and Application 2 minutes

This may seem overly detailed; however, I have found after teaching this method to hundreds of people that they appreciate the guidelines. I encourage those who begin using the method to keep track of how much time they spend on each step the first week that they do it. This will give you a feel for where you would like to make adjustments. Feel free to spend more time or less in a specific area and suit it to your own needs.

Devotional Journal

Meditation

What did God show me about Himself?

What verse or truth from my two Bible readings will I meditate on day and night?

Application

What did God, through His Word, tell me to do?

Other Thoughts

Devotional Planner

Date: ________________

Preparation

Prayer ◆ Song ◆ Reading of a Christian book

My Plan Today:

Confession

- Confession of known sin

My Plan Today:

Search Me, O God

Revelation

- Reading to know God through one Bible passage

My Plan Today:

Adoration

- Prayer and songs of praise
- Prayer and songs of thanksgiving
- Praying the names of God

My Plan Today:

Transformation

- Interactive reading and prayer of one chapter from Psalms or Proverbs

My Plan Today:

Communication

- Prayer for personal needs
- Prayer for needs of others
- Prayer of casting cares upon the Lord
- Prayer of claiming a promise from God

My Plan Today:

Devotional Journal

Meditation

What did God show me about Himself?

What verse or truth from my two Bible readings will I meditate on day and night?

Application

What did God, through His Word, tell me to do?

Other Thoughts

Devotional Planner

Date: ____________________

Preparation

Prayer ◆ Song ◆ Reading of a Christian book

My Plan Today:

Confession

- Confession of known sin

My Plan Today:

Search Me, O God

Revelation

- Reading to know God through one Bible passage

My Plan Today:

Adoration

- Prayer and songs of praise
- Prayer and songs of thanksgiving
- Praying the names of God

My Plan Today:

Transformation

- Interactive reading and prayer of one chapter from Psalms or Proverbs

My Plan Today:

Communication

- Prayer for personal needs
- Prayer for needs of others
- Prayer of casting cares upon the Lord
- Prayer of claiming a promise from God

My Plan Today:

Devotional Journal

Meditation

What did God show me about Himself?

What verse or truth from my two Bible readings will I meditate on day and night?

Application

What did God, through His Word, tell me to do?

Other Thoughts

Devotional Planner

Date: ________________

Preparation

Prayer ◆ Song ◆ Reading of a Christian book

My Plan Today:

Confession

- Confession of known sin

My Plan Today:

Search Me, O God

Revelation

- Reading to know God through one Bible passage

My Plan Today:

Adoration

- Prayer and songs of praise
- Prayer and songs of thanksgiving
- Praying the names of God

My Plan Today:

Transformation

- Interactive reading and prayer of one chapter from Psalms or Proverbs

My Plan Today:

Communication

- Prayer for personal needs
- Prayer for needs of others
- Prayer of casting cares upon the Lord
- Prayer of claiming a promise from God

My Plan Today:

Devotional Journal

Meditation

What did God show me about Himself?

What verse or truth from my two Bible readings will I meditate on day and night?

Application

What did God, through His Word, tell me to do?

Other Thoughts

Devotional Planner

Date: ______________

Preparation

Prayer ◆ Song ◆ Reading of a Christian book

My Plan Today:

Confession

- Confession of known sin

My Plan Today:

Search Me, O God

Revelation

- Reading to know God through one Bible passage

My Plan Today:

Adoration

- Prayer and songs of praise
- Prayer and songs of thanksgiving
- Praying the names of God

My Plan Today:

Transformation

- Interactive reading and prayer of one chapter from Psalms or Proverbs

My Plan Today:

Communication

- Prayer for personal needs
- Prayer for needs of others
- Prayer of casting cares upon the Lord
- Prayer of claiming a promise from God

My Plan Today:

Devotional Journal

Meditation

What did God show me about Himself?

What verse or truth from my two Bible readings will I meditate on day and night?

Application

What did God, through His Word, tell me to do?

Other Thoughts

Devotional Planner

Date: ______________

Preparation

Prayer ◆ Song ◆ Reading of a Christian book

My Plan Today:

Confession

- Confession of known sin

My Plan Today:

Search Me, O God

Revelation

- Reading to know God through one Bible passage

My Plan Today:

Adoration

- Prayer and songs of praise
- Prayer and songs of thanksgiving
- Praying the names of God

My Plan Today:

Transformation

- Interactive reading and prayer of one chapter from Psalms or Proverbs

My Plan Today:

Communication

- Prayer for personal needs
- Prayer for needs of others
- Prayer of casting cares upon the Lord
- Prayer of claiming a promise from God

My Plan Today:

Devotional Journal

Meditation

What did God show me about Himself?

What verse or truth from my two Bible readings will I meditate on day and night?

Application

What did God, through His Word, tell me to do?

Other Thoughts

Devotional Planner

Date: ________________

Preparation

Prayer ◆ Song ◆ Reading of a Christian book

My Plan Today:

Confession

- Confession of known sin

My Plan Today:

Search Me, O God

Revelation

- Reading to know God through one Bible passage

My Plan Today:

Adoration

- Prayer and songs of praise
- Prayer and songs of thanksgiving
- Praying the names of God

My Plan Today:

Transformation

- Interactive reading and prayer of one chapter from Psalms or Proverbs

My Plan Today:

Communication

- Prayer for personal needs
- Prayer for needs of others
- Prayer of casting cares upon the Lord
- Prayer of claiming a promise from God

My Plan Today:

Devotional Journal

Meditation

What did God show me about Himself?

What verse or truth from my two Bible readings will I meditate on day and night?

Application

What did God, through His Word, tell me to do?

Other Thoughts

Devotional Planner

Date: ____________________

Preparation

Prayer ◆ Song ◆ Reading of a Christian book

My Plan Today:

Confession

- Confession of known sin

My Plan Today:

Search Me, O God

Revelation

- Reading to know God through one Bible passage

My Plan Today:

Adoration

- Prayer and songs of praise
- Prayer and songs of thanksgiving
- Praying the names of God

My Plan Today:

Transformation

- Interactive reading and prayer of one chapter from Psalms or Proverbs

My Plan Today:

Communication

- Prayer for personal needs
- Prayer for needs of others
- Prayer of casting cares upon the Lord
- Prayer of claiming a promise from God

My Plan Today:

Devotional Journal

Meditation

What did God show me about Himself?

What verse or truth from my two Bible readings will I meditate on day and night?

Application

What did God, through His Word, tell me to do?

Other Thoughts

Devotional Planner

Date: ____________

Preparation

Prayer ◆ Song ◆ Reading of a Christian book

My Plan Today:

Confession

- Confession of known sin

My Plan Today:

Search Me, O God

Revelation

- Reading to know God through one Bible passage

My Plan Today:

Adoration

- Prayer and songs of praise
- Prayer and songs of thanksgiving
- Praying the names of God

My Plan Today:

Transformation

- Interactive reading and prayer of one chapter from Psalms or Proverbs

My Plan Today:

Communication

- Prayer for personal needs
- Prayer for needs of others
- Prayer of casting cares upon the Lord
- Prayer of claiming a promise from God

My Plan Today:

Devotional Journal

Meditation

What did God show me about Himself?

What verse or truth from my two Bible readings will I meditate on day and night?

Application

What did God, through His Word, tell me to do?

Other Thoughts

Devotional Planner

Date: ____________________

Preparation

Prayer ◆ Song ◆ Reading of a Christian book

My Plan Today:

Confession

- Confession of known sin

My Plan Today:

Search Me, O God

Revelation

- Reading to know God through one Bible passage

My Plan Today:

Adoration

- Prayer and songs of praise
- Prayer and songs of thanksgiving
- Praying the names of God

My Plan Today:

Transformation

- Interactive reading and prayer of one chapter from Psalms or Proverbs

My Plan Today:

Communication

- Prayer for personal needs
- Prayer for needs of others
- Prayer of casting cares upon the Lord
- Prayer of claiming a promise from God

My Plan Today:

Devotional Journal

Meditation

What did God show me about Himself?

What verse or truth from my two Bible readings will I meditate on day and night?

Application

What did God, through His Word, tell me to do?

Other Thoughts

Devotional Planner

Date: ____________

Preparation

Prayer ◆ Song ◆ Reading of a Christian book

My Plan Today:

Confession

- Confession of known sin

My Plan Today:

Search Me, O God

Revelation

- Reading to know God through one Bible passage

My Plan Today:

Adoration

- Prayer and songs of praise
- Prayer and songs of thanksgiving
- Praying the names of God

My Plan Today:

Transformation

- Interactive reading and prayer of one chapter from Psalms or Proverbs

My Plan Today:

Communication

- Prayer for personal needs
- Prayer for needs of others
- Prayer of casting cares upon the Lord
- Prayer of claiming a promise from God

My Plan Today:

Devotional Journal

Meditation

What did God show me about Himself?

What verse or truth from my two Bible readings will I meditate on day and night?

Application

What did God, through His Word, tell me to do?

Other Thoughts

Devotional Planner

Date: ____________________

Preparation

Prayer ◆ Song ◆ Reading of a Christian book

My Plan Today:

Confession

- Confession of known sin

My Plan Today:

Search Me, O God

Revelation

- Reading to know God through one Bible passage

My Plan Today:

Adoration

- Prayer and songs of praise
- Prayer and songs of thanksgiving
- Praying the names of God

My Plan Today:

Transformation

- Interactive reading and prayer of one chapter from Psalms or Proverbs

My Plan Today:

Communication

- Prayer for personal needs
- Prayer for needs of others
- Prayer of casting cares upon the Lord
- Prayer of claiming a promise from God

My Plan Today:

Devotional Journal

Meditation

What did God show me about Himself?

What verse or truth from my two Bible readings will I meditate on day and night?

Application

What did God, through His Word, tell me to do?

Other Thoughts

Devotional Planner

Date: ____________________

Preparation

Prayer ◆ Song ◆ Reading of a Christian book

My Plan Today:

Confession

- Confession of known sin

My Plan Today:

Search Me, O God

Revelation

- Reading to know God through one Bible passage

My Plan Today:

Adoration

- Prayer and songs of praise
- Prayer and songs of thanksgiving
- Praying the names of God

My Plan Today:

Transformation

- Interactive reading and prayer of one chapter from Psalms or Proverbs

My Plan Today:

Communication

- Prayer for personal needs
- Prayer for needs of others
- Prayer of casting cares upon the Lord
- Prayer of claiming a promise from God

My Plan Today:

Devotional Journal

Meditation

What did God show me about Himself?

What verse or truth from my two Bible readings will I meditate on day and night?

Application

What did God, through His Word, tell me to do?

Other Thoughts

Devotional Planner

Date: ____________

Preparation

Prayer ◆ Song ◆ Reading of a Christian book

My Plan Today:

Confession

- Confession of known sin

My Plan Today:

Search Me, O God

Revelation

- Reading to know God through one Bible passage

My Plan Today:

Adoration

- Prayer and songs of praise
- Prayer and songs of thanksgiving
- Praying the names of God

My Plan Today:

Transformation

- Interactive reading and prayer of one chapter from Psalms or Proverbs

My Plan Today:

Communication

- Prayer for personal needs
- Prayer for needs of others
- Prayer of casting cares upon the Lord
- Prayer of claiming a promise from God

My Plan Today:

Devotional Journal

Meditation

What did God show me about Himself?

What verse or truth from my two Bible readings will I meditate on day and night?

Application

What did God, through His Word, tell me to do?

Other Thoughts

Devotional Planner

Date: ____________________

Preparation

Prayer ◆ Song ◆ Reading of a Christian book

My Plan Today:

Confession

- Confession of known sin

My Plan Today:

Search Me, O God

Revelation

- Reading to know God through one Bible passage

My Plan Today:

Adoration

- Prayer and songs of praise
- Prayer and songs of thanksgiving
- Praying the names of God

My Plan Today:

Transformation

- Interactive reading and prayer of one chapter from Psalms or Proverbs

My Plan Today:

Communication

- Prayer for personal needs
- Prayer for needs of others
- Prayer of casting cares upon the Lord
- Prayer of claiming a promise from God

My Plan Today:

Devotional Journal

Meditation

What did God show me about Himself?

What verse or truth from my two Bible readings will I meditate on day and night?

Application

What did God, through His Word, tell me to do?

Other Thoughts

Devotional Planner

Date: ____________________

Preparation

Prayer ◆ Song ◆ Reading of a Christian book

My Plan Today:

Confession

- Confession of known sin

My Plan Today:

Search Me, O God

Revelation

- Reading to know God through one Bible passage

My Plan Today:

Adoration

- Prayer and songs of praise
- Prayer and songs of thanksgiving
- Praying the names of God

My Plan Today:

Transformation

- Interactive reading and prayer of one chapter from Psalms or Proverbs

My Plan Today:

Communication

- Prayer for personal needs
- Prayer for needs of others
- Prayer of casting cares upon the Lord
- Prayer of claiming a promise from God

My Plan Today:

Devotional Journal

Meditation

What did God show me about Himself?

What verse or truth from my two Bible readings will I meditate on day and night?

Application

What did God, through His Word, tell me to do?

Other Thoughts

Devotional Planner

Date: ____________________

Preparation

Prayer ◆ Song ◆ Reading of a Christian book

My Plan Today:

Confession

- Confession of known sin

My Plan Today:

Search Me, O God

Revelation

- Reading to know God through one Bible passage

My Plan Today:

Adoration

- Prayer and songs of praise
- Prayer and songs of thanksgiving
- Praying the names of God

My Plan Today:

Transformation

- Interactive reading and prayer of one chapter from Psalms or Proverbs

My Plan Today:

Communication

- Prayer for personal needs
- Prayer for needs of others
- Prayer of casting cares upon the Lord
- Prayer of claiming a promise from God

My Plan Today:

Devotional Journal

Meditation

What did God show me about Himself?

What verse or truth from my two Bible readings will I meditate on day and night?

Application

What did God, through His Word, tell me to do?

Other Thoughts

Devotional Planner

Date: ____________________

Preparation

Prayer ◆ Song ◆ Reading of a Christian book

My Plan Today:

Confession

- Confession of known sin

My Plan Today:

Search Me, O God

Revelation

- Reading to know God through one Bible passage

My Plan Today:

Adoration

- Prayer and songs of praise
- Prayer and songs of thanksgiving
- Praying the names of God

My Plan Today:

Transformation

- Interactive reading and prayer of one chapter from Psalms or Proverbs

My Plan Today:

Communication

- Prayer for personal needs
- Prayer for needs of others
- Prayer of casting cares upon the Lord
- Prayer of claiming a promise from God

My Plan Today:

Devotional Journal

Meditation

What did God show me about Himself?

What verse or truth from my two Bible readings will I meditate on day and night?

Application

What did God, through His Word, tell me to do?

Other Thoughts

Devotional Planner

Date: ____________________

Preparation

Prayer ◆ Song ◆ Reading of a Christian book

My Plan Today:

Confession

- Confession of known sin

My Plan Today:

Search Me, O God

Revelation

- Reading to know God through one Bible passage

My Plan Today:

Adoration

- Prayer and songs of praise
- Prayer and songs of thanksgiving
- Praying the names of God

My Plan Today:

Transformation

- Interactive reading and prayer of one chapter from Psalms or Proverbs

My Plan Today:

Communication

- Prayer for personal needs
- Prayer for needs of others
- Prayer of casting cares upon the Lord
- Prayer of claiming a promise from God

My Plan Today:

Devotional Journal

Meditation

What did God show me about Himself?

What verse or truth from my two Bible readings will I meditate on day and night?

Application

What did God, through His Word, tell me to do?

Other Thoughts

Devotional Planner

Date: ____________

Preparation

Prayer ◆ Song ◆ Reading of a Christian book

My Plan Today:

Confession

- Confession of known sin

My Plan Today:

Search Me, O God

Revelation

- Reading to know God through one Bible passage

My Plan Today:

Adoration

- Prayer and songs of praise
- Prayer and songs of thanksgiving
- Praying the names of God

My Plan Today:

Transformation

- Interactive reading and prayer of one chapter from Psalms or Proverbs

My Plan Today:

Communication

- Prayer for personal needs
- Prayer for needs of others
- Prayer of casting cares upon the Lord
- Prayer of claiming a promise from God

My Plan Today:

Devotional Journal

Meditation

What did God show me about Himself?

What verse or truth from my two Bible readings will I meditate on day and night?

Application

What did God, through His Word, tell me to do?

Other Thoughts

Devotional Planner

Date: ____________________

Preparation

Prayer ◆ Song ◆ Reading of a Christian book

My Plan Today:

Confession

- Confession of known sin

My Plan Today:

Search Me, O God

Revelation

- Reading to know God through one Bible passage

My Plan Today:

Adoration

- Prayer and songs of praise
- Prayer and songs of thanksgiving
- Praying the names of God

My Plan Today:

Transformation

- Interactive reading and prayer of one chapter from Psalms or Proverbs

My Plan Today:

Communication

- Prayer for personal needs
- Prayer for needs of others
- Prayer of casting cares upon the Lord
- Prayer of claiming a promise from God

My Plan Today:

Devotional Journal

Meditation

What did God show me about Himself?

What verse or truth from my two Bible readings will I meditate on day and night?

Application

What did God, through His Word, tell me to do?

Other Thoughts

Devotional Planner

Date: ____________

Preparation

Prayer ◆ Song ◆ Reading of a Christian book

My Plan Today:

Confession

- Confession of known sin

My Plan Today:

Search Me, O God

Revelation

- Reading to know God through one Bible passage

My Plan Today:

Adoration

- Prayer and songs of praise
- Prayer and songs of thanksgiving
- Praying the names of God

My Plan Today:

Transformation

- Interactive reading and prayer of one chapter from Psalms or Proverbs

My Plan Today:

Communication

- Prayer for personal needs
- Prayer for needs of others
- Prayer of casting cares upon the Lord
- Prayer of claiming a promise from God

My Plan Today:

Devotional Journal

Meditation

What did God show me about Himself?

What verse or truth from my two Bible readings will I meditate on day and night?

Application

What did God, through His Word, tell me to do?

Other Thoughts

Devotional Planner

Date: ____________________

Preparation

Prayer ◆ Song ◆ Reading of a Christian book

My Plan Today:

Confession

- Confession of known sin

My Plan Today:

Search Me, O God

Revelation

- Reading to know God through one Bible passage

My Plan Today:

Adoration

- Prayer and songs of praise
- Prayer and songs of thanksgiving
- Praying the names of God

My Plan Today:

Transformation

- Interactive reading and prayer of one chapter from Psalms or Proverbs

My Plan Today:

Communication

- Prayer for personal needs
- Prayer for needs of others
- Prayer of casting cares upon the Lord
- Prayer of claiming a promise from God

My Plan Today:

Devotional Journal

Meditation

What did God show me about Himself?

What verse or truth from my two Bible readings will I meditate on day and night?

Application

What did God, through His Word, tell me to do?

Other Thoughts

Devotional Planner

Date: ____________________

Preparation

Prayer ◆ Song ◆ Reading of a Christian book

My Plan Today:

Confession

- Confession of known sin

My Plan Today:

Search Me, O God

Revelation

- Reading to know God through one Bible passage

My Plan Today:

Adoration

- Prayer and songs of praise
- Prayer and songs of thanksgiving
- Praying the names of God

My Plan Today:

Transformation

- Interactive reading and prayer of one chapter from Psalms or Proverbs

My Plan Today:

Communication

- Prayer for personal needs
- Prayer for needs of others
- Prayer of casting cares upon the Lord
- Prayer of claiming a promise from God

My Plan Today:

Devotional Journal

Meditation

What did God show me about Himself?

What verse or truth from my two Bible readings will I meditate on day and night?

Application

What did God, through His Word, tell me to do?

Other Thoughts

Devotional Planner

Date: ________________

Preparation

Prayer ◆ Song ◆ Reading of a Christian book

My Plan Today:

Confession

- Confession of known sin

My Plan Today:

Search Me, O God

Revelation

- Reading to know God through one Bible passage

My Plan Today:

Adoration

- Prayer and songs of praise
- Prayer and songs of thanksgiving
- Praying the names of God

My Plan Today:

Transformation

- Interactive reading and prayer of one chapter from Psalms or Proverbs

My Plan Today:

Communication

- Prayer for personal needs
- Prayer for needs of others
- Prayer of casting cares upon the Lord
- Prayer of claiming a promise from God

My Plan Today:

Devotional Journal

Meditation

What did God show me about Himself?

What verse or truth from my two Bible readings will I meditate on day and night?

Application

What did God, through His Word, tell me to do?

Other Thoughts

Devotional Planner

Date: ____________________

Preparation

Prayer ◆ Song ◆ Reading of a Christian book

My Plan Today:

Confession

- Confession of known sin

My Plan Today:

Search Me, O God

Revelation

- Reading to know God through one Bible passage

My Plan Today:

Adoration

- Prayer and songs of praise
- Prayer and songs of thanksgiving
- Praying the names of God

My Plan Today:

Transformation

- Interactive reading and prayer of one chapter from Psalms or Proverbs

My Plan Today:

Communication

- Prayer for personal needs
- Prayer for needs of others
- Prayer of casting cares upon the Lord
- Prayer of claiming a promise from God

My Plan Today:

Devotional Journal

Meditation

What did God show me about Himself?

What verse or truth from my two Bible readings will I meditate on day and night?

Application

What did God, through His Word, tell me to do?

Other Thoughts

Devotional Planner

Date: ____________________

Preparation

Prayer ◆ Song ◆ Reading of a Christian book

My Plan Today:

Confession

- Confession of known sin

My Plan Today:

Search Me, O God

Revelation

- Reading to know God through one Bible passage

My Plan Today:

Adoration

- Prayer and songs of praise
- Prayer and songs of thanksgiving
- Praying the names of God

My Plan Today:

Transformation

- Interactive reading and prayer of one chapter from Psalms or Proverbs

My Plan Today:

Communication

- Prayer for personal needs
- Prayer for needs of others
- Prayer of casting cares upon the Lord
- Prayer of claiming a promise from God

My Plan Today:

Devotional Journal

Meditation

What did God show me about Himself?

What verse or truth from my two Bible readings will I meditate on day and night?

Application

What did God, through His Word, tell me to do?

Other Thoughts

Devotional Planner

Date: ______________

Preparation

Prayer ◆ Song ◆ Reading of a Christian book

My Plan Today:

Confession

- Confession of known sin

My Plan Today:

Search Me, O God

Revelation

- Reading to know God through one Bible passage

My Plan Today:

Adoration

- Prayer and songs of praise
- Prayer and songs of thanksgiving
- Praying the names of God

My Plan Today:

Transformation

- Interactive reading and prayer of one chapter from Psalms or Proverbs

My Plan Today:

Communication

- Prayer for personal needs
- Prayer for needs of others
- Prayer of casting cares upon the Lord
- Prayer of claiming a promise from God

My Plan Today:

Devotional Journal

Meditation

What did God show me about Himself?

What verse or truth from my two Bible readings will I meditate on day and night?

Application

What did God, through His Word, tell me to do?

Other Thoughts

Devotional Planner

Date: ____________________

Preparation

Prayer ◆ Song ◆ Reading of a Christian book

My Plan Today:

Confession

- Confession of known sin

My Plan Today:

Search Me, O God

Revelation

- Reading to know God through one Bible passage

My Plan Today:

Adoration

- Prayer and songs of praise
- Prayer and songs of thanksgiving
- Praying the names of God

My Plan Today:

Transformation

- Interactive reading and prayer of one chapter from Psalms or Proverbs

My Plan Today:

Communication

- Prayer for personal needs
- Prayer for needs of others
- Prayer of casting cares upon the Lord
- Prayer of claiming a promise from God

My Plan Today:

Devotional Journal

Meditation

What did God show me about Himself?

What verse or truth from my two Bible readings will I meditate on day and night?

Application

What did God, through His Word, tell me to do?

Other Thoughts

Devotional Planner

Date: ____________

Preparation

Prayer ◆ Song ◆ Reading of a Christian book

My Plan Today:

Confession

- Confession of known sin

My Plan Today:

Search Me, O God

Revelation

- Reading to know God through one Bible passage

My Plan Today:

Adoration

- Prayer and songs of praise
- Prayer and songs of thanksgiving
- Praying the names of God

My Plan Today:

Transformation

- Interactive reading and prayer of one chapter from Psalms or Proverbs

My Plan Today:

Communication

- Prayer for personal needs
- Prayer for needs of others
- Prayer of casting cares upon the Lord
- Prayer of claiming a promise from God

My Plan Today:

Devotional Journal

Meditation

What did God show me about Himself?

What verse or truth from my two Bible readings will I meditate on day and night?

Application

What did God, through His Word, tell me to do?

Other Thoughts

Devotional Planner

Date: ____________________

Preparation

Prayer ◆ Song ◆ Reading of a Christian book

My Plan Today:

Confession

- Confession of known sin

My Plan Today:

Search Me, O God

Revelation

- Reading to know God through one Bible passage

My Plan Today:

Adoration

- Prayer and songs of praise
- Prayer and songs of thanksgiving
- Praying the names of God

My Plan Today:

Transformation

- Interactive reading and prayer of one chapter from Psalms or Proverbs

My Plan Today:

Communication

- Prayer for personal needs
- Prayer for needs of others
- Prayer of casting cares upon the Lord
- Prayer of claiming a promise from God

My Plan Today:

Devotional Journal

Meditation

What did God show me about Himself?

What verse or truth from my two Bible readings will I meditate on day and night?

Application

What did God, through His Word, tell me to do?

Other Thoughts

Devotional Planner

Date: ____________________

Preparation

Prayer ◆ Song ◆ Reading of a Christian book

My Plan Today:

Confession

- Confession of known sin

My Plan Today:

Search Me, O God

Revelation

- Reading to know God through one Bible passage

My Plan Today:

Adoration

- Prayer and songs of praise
- Prayer and songs of thanksgiving
- Praying the names of God

My Plan Today:

Transformation

- Interactive reading and prayer of one chapter from Psalms or Proverbs

My Plan Today:

Communication

- Prayer for personal needs
- Prayer for needs of others
- Prayer of casting cares upon the Lord
- Prayer of claiming a promise from God

My Plan Today:

Devotional Journal

Meditation

What did God show me about Himself?

What verse or truth from my two Bible readings will I meditate on day and night?

Application

What did God, through His Word, tell me to do?

Other Thoughts

Devotional Planner

Date: ____________________

Preparation

Prayer ◆ Song ◆ Reading of a Christian book

My Plan Today:

Confession

- Confession of known sin

My Plan Today:

Search Me, O God

Revelation

- Reading to know God through one Bible passage

My Plan Today:

Adoration

- Prayer and songs of praise
- Prayer and songs of thanksgiving
- Praying the names of God

My Plan Today:

Transformation

- Interactive reading and prayer of one chapter from Psalms or Proverbs

My Plan Today:

Communication

- Prayer for personal needs
- Prayer for needs of others
- Prayer of casting cares upon the Lord
- Prayer of claiming a promise from God

My Plan Today:

Devotional Journal

Meditation

What did God show me about Himself?

What verse or truth from my two Bible readings will I meditate on day and night?

Application

What did God, through His Word, tell me to do?

Other Thoughts

Devotional Planner

Date: ____________________

Preparation

Prayer ◆ Song ◆ Reading of a Christian book

My Plan Today:

Confession

- Confession of known sin

My Plan Today:

Search Me, O God

Revelation

- Reading to know God through one Bible passage

My Plan Today:

Adoration

- Prayer and songs of praise
- Prayer and songs of thanksgiving
- Praying the names of God

My Plan Today:

Transformation

- Interactive reading and prayer of one chapter from Psalms or Proverbs

My Plan Today:

Communication

- Prayer for personal needs
- Prayer for needs of others
- Prayer of casting cares upon the Lord
- Prayer of claiming a promise from God

My Plan Today:

Devotional Journal

Meditation

What did God show me about Himself?

What verse or truth from my two Bible readings will I meditate on day and night?

Application

What did God, through His Word, tell me to do?

Other Thoughts

Devotional Planner

Date: ____________________

Preparation

Prayer ◆ Song ◆ Reading of a Christian book

My Plan Today:

Confession

- Confession of known sin

My Plan Today:

Search Me, O God

Revelation

- Reading to know God through one Bible passage

My Plan Today:

Adoration

- Prayer and songs of praise
- Prayer and songs of thanksgiving
- Praying the names of God

My Plan Today:

Transformation

- Interactive reading and prayer of one chapter from Psalms or Proverbs

My Plan Today:

Communication

- Prayer for personal needs
- Prayer for needs of others
- Prayer of casting cares upon the Lord
- Prayer of claiming a promise from God

My Plan Today:

Devotional Journal

Meditation

What did God show me about Himself?

What verse or truth from my two Bible readings will I meditate on day and night?

Application

What did God, through His Word, tell me to do?

Other Thoughts

Devotional Planner

Date: ____________________

Preparation

Prayer ◆ Song ◆ Reading of a Christian book

My Plan Today:

Confession

- Confession of known sin

My Plan Today:

Search Me, O God

Revelation

- Reading to know God through one Bible passage

My Plan Today:

Adoration

- Prayer and songs of praise
- Prayer and songs of thanksgiving
- Praying the names of God

My Plan Today:

Transformation

- Interactive reading and prayer of one chapter from Psalms or Proverbs

My Plan Today:

Communication

- Prayer for personal needs
- Prayer for needs of others
- Prayer of casting cares upon the Lord
- Prayer of claiming a promise from God

My Plan Today:

Devotional Journal

Meditation

What did God show me about Himself?

What verse or truth from my two Bible readings will I meditate on day and night?

Application

What did God, through His Word, tell me to do?

Other Thoughts

Devotional Planner

Date: ____________________

Preparation

Prayer ◆ Song ◆ Reading of a Christian book

My Plan Today:

Confession

- Confession of known sin

My Plan Today:

Search Me, O God

Revelation

- Reading to know God through one Bible passage

My Plan Today:

Adoration

- Prayer and songs of praise
- Prayer and songs of thanksgiving
- Praying the names of God

My Plan Today:

Transformation

- Interactive reading and prayer of one chapter from Psalms or Proverbs

My Plan Today:

Communication

- Prayer for personal needs
- Prayer for needs of others
- Prayer of casting cares upon the Lord
- Prayer of claiming a promise from God

My Plan Today:

Devotional Journal

Meditation

What did God show me about Himself?

What verse or truth from my two Bible readings will I meditate on day and night?

Application

What did God, through His Word, tell me to do?

Other Thoughts

Devotional Planner

Date: ____________________

Preparation

Prayer ◆ Song ◆ Reading of a Christian book

My Plan Today:

Confession

- Confession of known sin

My Plan Today:

Search Me, O God

Revelation

- Reading to know God through one Bible passage

My Plan Today:

Adoration

- Prayer and songs of praise
- Prayer and songs of thanksgiving
- Praying the names of God

My Plan Today:

Transformation

- Interactive reading and prayer of one chapter from Psalms or Proverbs

My Plan Today:

Communication

- Prayer for personal needs
- Prayer for needs of others
- Prayer of casting cares upon the Lord
- Prayer of claiming a promise from God

My Plan Today:

Devotional Journal

Meditation

What did God show me about Himself?

What verse or truth from my two Bible readings will I meditate on day and night?

Application

What did God, through His Word, tell me to do?

Other Thoughts

Devotional Planner

Date: ____________________

Preparation

Prayer ◆ Song ◆ Reading of a Christian book

My Plan Today:

Confession

- Confession of known sin

My Plan Today:

Search Me, O God

Revelation

- Reading to know God through one Bible passage

My Plan Today:

Adoration

- Prayer and songs of praise
- Prayer and songs of thanksgiving
- Praying the names of God

My Plan Today:

Transformation

- Interactive reading and prayer of one chapter from Psalms or Proverbs

My Plan Today:

Communication

- Prayer for personal needs
- Prayer for needs of others
- Prayer of casting cares upon the Lord
- Prayer of claiming a promise from God

My Plan Today:

Devotional Journal

Meditation

What did God show me about Himself?

What verse or truth from my two Bible readings will I meditate on day and night?

Application

What did God, through His Word, tell me to do?

Other Thoughts

Devotional Planner

Date: ____________

Preparation

Prayer ◆ Song ◆ Reading of a Christian book

My Plan Today:

Confession

- Confession of known sin

My Plan Today:

Search Me, O God

Revelation

- Reading to know God through one Bible passage

My Plan Today:

Adoration

- Prayer and songs of praise
- Prayer and songs of thanksgiving
- Praying the names of God

My Plan Today:

Transformation

- Interactive reading and prayer of one chapter from Psalms or Proverbs

My Plan Today:

Communication

- Prayer for personal needs
- Prayer for needs of others
- Prayer of casting cares upon the Lord
- Prayer of claiming a promise from God

My Plan Today:

Devotional Journal

Meditation

What did God show me about Himself?

What verse or truth from my two Bible readings will I meditate on day and night?

Application

What did God, through His Word, tell me to do?

Other Thoughts

Devotional Planner

Date: ____________________

Preparation

Prayer ◆ Song ◆ Reading of a Christian book

My Plan Today:

Confession

- Confession of known sin

My Plan Today:

Search Me, O God

Revelation

- Reading to know God through one Bible passage

My Plan Today:

Adoration

- Prayer and songs of praise
- Prayer and songs of thanksgiving
- Praying the names of God

My Plan Today:

Transformation

- Interactive reading and prayer of one chapter from Psalms or Proverbs

My Plan Today:

Communication

- Prayer for personal needs
- Prayer for needs of others
- Prayer of casting cares upon the Lord
- Prayer of claiming a promise from God

My Plan Today:

Devotional Journal

Meditation

What did God show me about Himself?

What verse or truth from my two Bible readings will I meditate on day and night?

Application

What did God, through His Word, tell me to do?

Other Thoughts

Devotional Planner

Date: ____________________

Preparation

Prayer ◆ Song ◆ Reading of a Christian book

My Plan Today:

Confession

- Confession of known sin

My Plan Today:

Search Me, O God

Revelation

- Reading to know God through one Bible passage

My Plan Today:

Adoration

- Prayer and songs of praise
- Prayer and songs of thanksgiving
- Praying the names of God

My Plan Today:

Transformation

- Interactive reading and prayer of one chapter from Psalms or Proverbs

My Plan Today:

Communication

- Prayer for personal needs
- Prayer for needs of others
- Prayer of casting cares upon the Lord
- Prayer of claiming a promise from God

My Plan Today:

Devotional Journal

Meditation

What did God show me about Himself?

What verse or truth from my two Bible readings will I meditate on day and night?

Application

What did God, through His Word, tell me to do?

Other Thoughts

Devotional Planner

Date: ________________

Preparation

Prayer ◆ Song ◆ Reading of a Christian book

My Plan Today:

Confession

- Confession of known sin

My Plan Today:

Search Me, O God

Revelation

- Reading to know God through one Bible passage

My Plan Today:

Adoration

- Prayer and songs of praise
- Prayer and songs of thanksgiving
- Praying the names of God

My Plan Today:

Transformation

- Interactive reading and prayer of one chapter from Psalms or Proverbs

My Plan Today:

Communication

- Prayer for personal needs
- Prayer for needs of others
- Prayer of casting cares upon the Lord
- Prayer of claiming a promise from God

My Plan Today:

Devotional Journal

Meditation

What did God show me about Himself?

What verse or truth from my two Bible readings will I meditate on day and night?

Application

What did God, through His Word, tell me to do?

Other Thoughts

Devotional Planner

Date: ____________________

Preparation

Prayer ◆ Song ◆ Reading of a Christian book

My Plan Today:

Confession

- Confession of known sin

My Plan Today:

Search Me, O God

Revelation

- Reading to know God through one Bible passage

My Plan Today:

Adoration

- Prayer and songs of praise
- Prayer and songs of thanksgiving
- Praying the names of God

My Plan Today:

Transformation

- Interactive reading and prayer of one chapter from Psalms or Proverbs

My Plan Today:

Communication

- Prayer for personal needs
- Prayer for needs of others
- Prayer of casting cares upon the Lord
- Prayer of claiming a promise from God

My Plan Today:

Devotional Journal

Meditation

What did God show me about Himself?

What verse or truth from my two Bible readings will I meditate on day and night?

Application

What did God, through His Word, tell me to do?

Other Thoughts

Devotional Planner

Date: ____________________

Preparation

Prayer ◆ Song ◆ Reading of a Christian book

My Plan Today:

Confession

- Confession of known sin

My Plan Today:

Search Me, O God

Revelation

- Reading to know God through one Bible passage

My Plan Today:

Adoration

- Prayer and songs of praise
- Prayer and songs of thanksgiving
- Praying the names of God

My Plan Today:

Transformation

- Interactive reading and prayer of one chapter from Psalms or Proverbs

My Plan Today:

Communication

- Prayer for personal needs
- Prayer for needs of others
- Prayer of casting cares upon the Lord
- Prayer of claiming a promise from God

My Plan Today:

Devotional Journal

Meditation

What did God show me about Himself?

What verse or truth from my two Bible readings will I meditate on day and night?

Application

What did God, through His Word, tell me to do?

Other Thoughts

Devotional Planner

Date: ____________

Preparation

Prayer ◆ Song ◆ Reading of a Christian book

My Plan Today:

Confession

- Confession of known sin

My Plan Today:

Search Me, O God

Revelation

- Reading to know God through one Bible passage

My Plan Today:

Adoration

- Prayer and songs of praise
- Prayer and songs of thanksgiving
- Praying the names of God

My Plan Today:

Transformation

- Interactive reading and prayer of one chapter from Psalms or Proverbs

My Plan Today:

Communication

- Prayer for personal needs
- Prayer for needs of others
- Prayer of casting cares upon the Lord
- Prayer of claiming a promise from God

My Plan Today:

Devotional Journal

Meditation

What did God show me about Himself?

What verse or truth from my two Bible readings will I meditate on day and night?

Application

What did God, through His Word, tell me to do?

Other Thoughts

Devotional Planner

Date: ____________________

Preparation

Prayer ◆ Song ◆ Reading of a Christian book

My Plan Today:

Confession

- Confession of known sin

My Plan Today:

Search Me, O God

Revelation

- Reading to know God through one Bible passage

My Plan Today:

Adoration

- Prayer and songs of praise
- Prayer and songs of thanksgiving
- Praying the names of God

My Plan Today:

Transformation

- Interactive reading and prayer of one chapter from Psalms or Proverbs

My Plan Today:

Communication

- Prayer for personal needs
- Prayer for needs of others
- Prayer of casting cares upon the Lord
- Prayer of claiming a promise from God

My Plan Today:

Devotional Journal

Meditation

What did God show me about Himself?

What verse or truth from my two Bible readings will I meditate on day and night?

Application

What did God, through His Word, tell me to do?

Other Thoughts

Devotional Planner

Date: ____________________

Preparation

Prayer ◆ Song ◆ Reading of a Christian book

My Plan Today:

Confession

- Confession of known sin

My Plan Today:

Search Me, O God

Revelation

- Reading to know God through one Bible passage

My Plan Today:

Adoration

- Prayer and songs of praise
- Prayer and songs of thanksgiving
- Praying the names of God

My Plan Today:

Transformation

- Interactive reading and prayer of one chapter from Psalms or Proverbs

My Plan Today:

Communication

- Prayer for personal needs
- Prayer for needs of others
- Prayer of casting cares upon the Lord
- Prayer of claiming a promise from God

My Plan Today:

Devotional Journal

Meditation

What did God show me about Himself?

What verse or truth from my two Bible readings will I meditate on day and night?

Application

What did God, through His Word, tell me to do?

Other Thoughts

Devotional Planner

Date: ____________________

Preparation

Prayer ◆ Song ◆ Reading of a Christian book

My Plan Today:

Confession

- Confession of known sin

My Plan Today:

Search Me, O God

Revelation

- Reading to know God through one Bible passage

My Plan Today:

Adoration

- Prayer and songs of praise
- Prayer and songs of thanksgiving
- Praying the names of God

My Plan Today:

Transformation

- Interactive reading and prayer of one chapter from Psalms or Proverbs

My Plan Today:

Communication

- Prayer for personal needs
- Prayer for needs of others
- Prayer of casting cares upon the Lord
- Prayer of claiming a promise from God

My Plan Today:

Devotional Journal

Meditation

What did God show me about Himself?

What verse or truth from my two Bible readings will I meditate on day and night?

Application

What did God, through His Word, tell me to do?

Other Thoughts

Devotional Planner

Date: ____________________

Preparation

Prayer ◆ Song ◆ Reading of a Christian book

My Plan Today:

Confession

- Confession of known sin

My Plan Today:

Search Me, O God

Revelation

- Reading to know God through one Bible passage

My Plan Today:

Adoration

- Prayer and songs of praise
- Prayer and songs of thanksgiving
- Praying the names of God

My Plan Today:

Transformation

- Interactive reading and prayer of one chapter from Psalms or Proverbs

My Plan Today:

Communication

- Prayer for personal needs
- Prayer for needs of others
- Prayer of casting cares upon the Lord
- Prayer of claiming a promise from God

My Plan Today:

Devotional Journal

Meditation

What did God show me about Himself?

What verse or truth from my two Bible readings will I meditate on day and night?

Application

What did God, through His Word, tell me to do?

Other Thoughts

Devotional Planner

Date: ___________________

Preparation

Prayer ◆ Song ◆ Reading of a Christian book

My Plan Today:

Confession

- Confession of known sin

My Plan Today:

Search Me, O God

Revelation

- Reading to know God through one Bible passage

My Plan Today:

Adoration

- Prayer and songs of praise
- Prayer and songs of thanksgiving
- Praying the names of God

My Plan Today:

Transformation

- Interactive reading and prayer of one chapter from Psalms or Proverbs

My Plan Today:

Communication

- Prayer for personal needs
- Prayer for needs of others
- Prayer of casting cares upon the Lord
- Prayer of claiming a promise from God

My Plan Today:

Devotional Journal

Meditation

What did God show me about Himself?

What verse or truth from my two Bible readings will I meditate on day and night?

Application

What did God, through His Word, tell me to do?

Other Thoughts

Devotional Planner

Date: ____________________

Preparation

Prayer ◆ Song ◆ Reading of a Christian book

My Plan Today:

Confession

- Confession of known sin

My Plan Today:

Search Me, O God

Revelation

- Reading to know God through one Bible passage

My Plan Today:

Adoration

- Prayer and songs of praise
- Prayer and songs of thanksgiving
- Praying the names of God

My Plan Today:

Transformation

- Interactive reading and prayer of one chapter from Psalms or Proverbs

My Plan Today:

Communication

- Prayer for personal needs
- Prayer for needs of others
- Prayer of casting cares upon the Lord
- Prayer of claiming a promise from God

My Plan Today:

Devotional Journal

Meditation

What did God show me about Himself?

What verse or truth from my two Bible readings will I meditate on day and night?

Application

What did God, through His Word, tell me to do?

Other Thoughts

Devotional Planner

Date: ____________________

Preparation

Prayer ◆ Song ◆ Reading of a Christian book

My Plan Today:

Confession

- Confession of known sin

My Plan Today:

Search Me, O God

Revelation

- Reading to know God through one Bible passage

My Plan Today:

Adoration

- Prayer and songs of praise
- Prayer and songs of thanksgiving
- Praying the names of God

My Plan Today:

Transformation

- Interactive reading and prayer of one chapter from Psalms or Proverbs

My Plan Today:

Communication

- Prayer for personal needs
- Prayer for needs of others
- Prayer of casting cares upon the Lord
- Prayer of claiming a promise from God

My Plan Today:

Devotional Journal

Meditation

What did God show me about Himself?

What verse or truth from my two Bible readings will I meditate on day and night?

Application

What did God, through His Word, tell me to do?

Other Thoughts

Devotional Planner

Date: ____________________

Preparation

Prayer ◆ Song ◆ Reading of a Christian book

My Plan Today:

Confession

- Confession of known sin

My Plan Today:

Search Me, O God

Revelation

- Reading to know God through one Bible passage

My Plan Today:

Adoration

- Prayer and songs of praise
- Prayer and songs of thanksgiving
- Praying the names of God

My Plan Today:

Transformation

- Interactive reading and prayer of one chapter from Psalms or Proverbs

My Plan Today:

Communication

- Prayer for personal needs
- Prayer for needs of others
- Prayer of casting cares upon the Lord
- Prayer of claiming a promise from God

My Plan Today:

Devotional Journal

Meditation

What did God show me about Himself?

What verse or truth from my two Bible readings will I meditate on day and night?

Application

What did God, through His Word, tell me to do?

Other Thoughts

Devotional Planner

Date: ____________________

Preparation

Prayer ◆ Song ◆ Reading of a Christian book

My Plan Today:

Confession

- Confession of known sin

My Plan Today:

Search Me, O God

Revelation

- Reading to know God through one Bible passage

My Plan Today:

Adoration

- Prayer and songs of praise
- Prayer and songs of thanksgiving
- Praying the names of God

My Plan Today:

Transformation

- Interactive reading and prayer of one chapter from Psalms or Proverbs

My Plan Today:

Communication

- Prayer for personal needs
- Prayer for needs of others
- Prayer of casting cares upon the Lord
- Prayer of claiming a promise from God

My Plan Today:

Devotional Journal

Meditation

What did God show me about Himself?

What verse or truth from my two Bible readings will I meditate on
day and night?

Application

What did God, through His Word, tell me to do?

Other Thoughts

Devotional Planner

Date: ____________

Preparation

Prayer ◆ Song ◆ Reading of a Christian book

My Plan Today:

Confession

- Confession of known sin

My Plan Today:

Search Me, O God

Revelation

- Reading to know God through one Bible passage

My Plan Today:

Adoration

- Prayer and songs of praise
- Prayer and songs of thanksgiving
- Praying the names of God

My Plan Today:

Transformation

- Interactive reading and prayer of one chapter from Psalms or Proverbs

My Plan Today:

Communication

- Prayer for personal needs
- Prayer for needs of others
- Prayer of casting cares upon the Lord
- Prayer of claiming a promise from God

My Plan Today:

Devotional Journal

Meditation

What did God show me about Himself?

What verse or truth from my two Bible readings will I meditate on day and night?

Application

What did God, through His Word, tell me to do?

Other Thoughts

Devotional Planner

Date: ____________

Preparation

Prayer ◆ Song ◆ Reading of a Christian book

My Plan Today:

Confession

- Confession of known sin

My Plan Today:

Search Me, O God

Revelation

- Reading to know God through one Bible passage

My Plan Today:

Adoration

- Prayer and songs of praise
- Prayer and songs of thanksgiving
- Praying the names of God

My Plan Today:

Transformation

- Interactive reading and prayer of one chapter from Psalms or Proverbs

My Plan Today:

Communication

- Prayer for personal needs
- Prayer for needs of others
- Prayer of casting cares upon the Lord
- Prayer of claiming a promise from God

My Plan Today:

Devotional Journal

Meditation

What did God show me about Himself?

What verse or truth from my two Bible readings will I meditate on day and night?

Application

What did God, through His Word, tell me to do?

Other Thoughts

Devotional Planner

Date: ______________

Preparation

Prayer ◆ Song ◆ Reading of a Christian book

My Plan Today:

Confession

- Confession of known sin

My Plan Today:

Search Me, O God

Revelation

- Reading to know God through one Bible passage

My Plan Today:

Adoration

- Prayer and songs of praise
- Prayer and songs of thanksgiving
- Praying the names of God

My Plan Today:

Transformation

- Interactive reading and prayer of one chapter from Psalms or Proverbs

My Plan Today:

Communication

- Prayer for personal needs
- Prayer for needs of others
- Prayer of casting cares upon the Lord
- Prayer of claiming a promise from God

My Plan Today:

Devotional Journal

Meditation

What did God show me about Himself?

What verse or truth from my two Bible readings will I meditate on
day and night?

Application

What did God, through His Word, tell me to do?

Other Thoughts

Devotional Planner

Date: ____________________

Preparation

Prayer ◆ Song ◆ Reading of a Christian book

My Plan Today:

Confession

- Confession of known sin

My Plan Today:

Search Me, O God

Revelation

- Reading to know God through one Bible passage

My Plan Today:

Adoration

- Prayer and songs of praise
- Prayer and songs of thanksgiving
- Praying the names of God

My Plan Today:

Transformation

- Interactive reading and prayer of one chapter from Psalms or Proverbs

My Plan Today:

Communication

- Prayer for personal needs
- Prayer for needs of others
- Prayer of casting cares upon the Lord
- Prayer of claiming a promise from God

My Plan Today:

Devotional Journal

Meditation

What did God show me about Himself?

What verse or truth from my two Bible readings will I meditate on day and night?

Application

What did God, through His Word, tell me to do?

Other Thoughts

Devotional Planner

Date: ____________________

Preparation

Prayer ◆ Song ◆ Reading of a Christian book

My Plan Today:

Confession

- Confession of known sin

My Plan Today:

Search Me, O God

Revelation

- Reading to know God through one Bible passage

My Plan Today:

Adoration

- Prayer and songs of praise
- Prayer and songs of thanksgiving
- Praying the names of God

My Plan Today:

Transformation

- Interactive reading and prayer of one chapter from Psalms or Proverbs

My Plan Today:

Communication

- Prayer for personal needs
- Prayer for needs of others
- Prayer of casting cares upon the Lord
- Prayer of claiming a promise from God

My Plan Today:

Devotional Journal

Meditation

What did God show me about Himself?

What verse or truth from my two Bible readings will I meditate on day and night?

Application

What did God, through His Word, tell me to do?

Other Thoughts

Devotional Planner

Date: ____________________

Preparation

Prayer ◆ Song ◆ Reading of a Christian book

My Plan Today:

Confession

- Confession of known sin

My Plan Today:

Search Me, O God

Revelation

- Reading to know God through one Bible passage

My Plan Today:

Adoration

- Prayer and songs of praise
- Prayer and songs of thanksgiving
- Praying the names of God

My Plan Today:

Transformation

- Interactive reading and prayer of one chapter from Psalms or Proverbs

My Plan Today:

Communication

- Prayer for personal needs
- Prayer for needs of others
- Prayer of casting cares upon the Lord
- Prayer of claiming a promise from God

My Plan Today:

Devotional Journal

Meditation

What did God show me about Himself?

What verse or truth from my two Bible readings will I meditate on day and night?

Application

What did God, through His Word, tell me to do?

Other Thoughts

Devotional Planner

Date: ____________________

Preparation

Prayer ◆ Song ◆ Reading of a Christian book

My Plan Today:

Confession

- Confession of known sin

My Plan Today:

Search Me, O God

Revelation

- Reading to know God through one Bible passage

My Plan Today:

Adoration

- Prayer and songs of praise
- Prayer and songs of thanksgiving
- Praying the names of God

My Plan Today:

Transformation

- Interactive reading and prayer of one chapter from Psalms or Proverbs

My Plan Today:

Communication

- Prayer for personal needs
- Prayer for needs of others
- Prayer of casting cares upon the Lord
- Prayer of claiming a promise from God

My Plan Today:

Devotional Journal

Meditation

What did God show me about Himself?

What verse or truth from my two Bible readings will I meditate on day and night?

Application

What did God, through His Word, tell me to do?

Other Thoughts

Devotional Planner

Date: ____________________

Preparation

Prayer ◆ Song ◆ Reading of a Christian book

My Plan Today:

Confession

- Confession of known sin

My Plan Today:

Search Me, O God

Revelation

- Reading to know God through one Bible passage

My Plan Today:

Adoration

- Prayer and songs of praise
- Prayer and songs of thanksgiving
- Praying the names of God

My Plan Today:

Transformation

- Interactive reading and prayer of one chapter from Psalms or Proverbs

My Plan Today:

Communication

- Prayer for personal needs
- Prayer for needs of others
- Prayer of casting cares upon the Lord
- Prayer of claiming a promise from God

My Plan Today:

Devotional Journal

Meditation

What did God show me about Himself?

What verse or truth from my two Bible readings will I meditate on day and night?

Application

What did God, through His Word, tell me to do?

Other Thoughts

Devotional Planner

Date: ____________________

Preparation

Prayer ◆ Song ◆ Reading of a Christian book

My Plan Today:

Confession

- Confession of known sin

My Plan Today:

Search Me, O God

Revelation

- Reading to know God through one Bible passage

My Plan Today:

Adoration

- Prayer and songs of praise
- Prayer and songs of thanksgiving
- Praying the names of God

My Plan Today:

Transformation

- Interactive reading and prayer of one chapter from Psalms or Proverbs

My Plan Today:

Communication

- Prayer for personal needs
- Prayer for needs of others
- Prayer of casting cares upon the Lord
- Prayer of claiming a promise from God

My Plan Today:

Devotional Journal

Meditation

What did God show me about Himself?

What verse or truth from my two Bible readings will I meditate on day and night?

Application

What did God, through His Word, tell me to do?

Other Thoughts

Devotional Planner

Date: ____________________

Preparation

Prayer ◆ Song ◆ Reading of a Christian book

My Plan Today:

Confession

- Confession of known sin

My Plan Today:

Search Me, O God

Revelation

- Reading to know God through one Bible passage

My Plan Today:

Adoration

- Prayer and songs of praise
- Prayer and songs of thanksgiving
- Praying the names of God

My Plan Today:

Transformation

- Interactive reading and prayer of one chapter from Psalms or Proverbs

My Plan Today:

Communication

- Prayer for personal needs
- Prayer for needs of others
- Prayer of casting cares upon the Lord
- Prayer of claiming a promise from God

My Plan Today:

Devotional Journal

Meditation

What did God show me about Himself?

What verse or truth from my two Bible readings will I meditate on day and night?

Application

What did God, through His Word, tell me to do?

Other Thoughts

Devotional Planner

Date: ____________________

Preparation

Prayer ◆ Song ◆ Reading of a Christian book

My Plan Today:

Confession

- Confession of known sin

My Plan Today:

Search Me, O God

Revelation

- Reading to know God through one Bible passage

My Plan Today:

Adoration

- Prayer and songs of praise
- Prayer and songs of thanksgiving
- Praying the names of God

My Plan Today:

Transformation

- Interactive reading and prayer of one chapter from Psalms or Proverbs

My Plan Today:

Communication

- Prayer for personal needs
- Prayer for needs of others
- Prayer of casting cares upon the Lord
- Prayer of claiming a promise from God

My Plan Today:

Devotional Journal

Meditation

What did God show me about Himself?

What verse or truth from my two Bible readings will I meditate on day and night?

Application

What did God, through His Word, tell me to do?

Other Thoughts

Devotional Planner

Date: ______________________

Preparation

Prayer ◆ Song ◆ Reading of a Christian book

My Plan Today:

Confession

- Confession of known sin

My Plan Today:

Search Me, O God

Revelation

- Reading to know God through one Bible passage

My Plan Today:

Adoration

- Prayer and songs of praise
- Prayer and songs of thanksgiving
- Praying the names of God

My Plan Today:

Transformation

- Interactive reading and prayer of one chapter from Psalms or Proverbs

My Plan Today:

Communication

- Prayer for personal needs
- Prayer for needs of others
- Prayer of casting cares upon the Lord
- Prayer of claiming a promise from God

My Plan Today:

Devotional Journal

Meditation

What did God show me about Himself?

What verse or truth from my two Bible readings will I meditate on day and night?

Application

What did God, through His Word, tell me to do?

Other Thoughts

Devotional Planner

Date: ____________

Preparation

Prayer ◆ Song ◆ Reading of a Christian book

My Plan Today:

Confession

- Confession of known sin

My Plan Today:

Search Me, O God

Revelation

- Reading to know God through one Bible passage

My Plan Today:

Adoration

- Prayer and songs of praise
- Prayer and songs of thanksgiving
- Praying the names of God

My Plan Today:

Transformation

- Interactive reading and prayer of one chapter from Psalms or Proverbs

My Plan Today:

Communication

- Prayer for personal needs
- Prayer for needs of others
- Prayer of casting cares upon the Lord
- Prayer of claiming a promise from God

My Plan Today:

Devotional Journal

Meditation

What did God show me about Himself?

What verse or truth from my two Bible readings will I meditate on day and night?

Application

What did God, through His Word, tell me to do?

Other Thoughts

Devotional Planner

Date: ________________

Preparation

Prayer ◆ Song ◆ Reading of a Christian book

My Plan Today:

Confession

- Confession of known sin

My Plan Today:

Search Me, O God

Revelation

- Reading to know God through one Bible passage

My Plan Today:

Adoration

- Prayer and songs of praise
- Prayer and songs of thanksgiving
- Praying the names of God

My Plan Today:

Transformation

- Interactive reading and prayer of one chapter from Psalms or Proverbs

My Plan Today:

Communication

- Prayer for personal needs
- Prayer for needs of others
- Prayer of casting cares upon the Lord
- Prayer of claiming a promise from God

My Plan Today:

Devotional Journal

Meditation

What did God show me about Himself?

What verse or truth from my two Bible readings will I meditate on day and night?

Application

What did God, through His Word, tell me to do?

Other Thoughts

Devotional Planner

Date: ____________________

Preparation

Prayer ◆ Song ◆ Reading of a Christian book

My Plan Today:

Confession

- Confession of known sin

My Plan Today:

Search Me, O God

Revelation

- Reading to know God through one Bible passage

My Plan Today:

Adoration

- Prayer and songs of praise
- Prayer and songs of thanksgiving
- Praying the names of God

My Plan Today:

Transformation

- Interactive reading and prayer of one chapter from Psalms or Proverbs

My Plan Today:

Communication

- Prayer for personal needs
- Prayer for needs of others
- Prayer of casting cares upon the Lord
- Prayer of claiming a promise from God

My Plan Today:

Devotional Journal

Meditation

What did God show me about Himself?

What verse or truth from my two Bible readings will I meditate on day and night?

Application

What did God, through His Word, tell me to do?

Other Thoughts

Devotional Planner

Date: ________________

Preparation

Prayer ◆ Song ◆ Reading of a Christian book

My Plan Today:

Confession

- Confession of known sin

My Plan Today:

Search Me, O God

Revelation

- Reading to know God through one Bible passage

My Plan Today:

Adoration

- Prayer and songs of praise
- Prayer and songs of thanksgiving
- Praying the names of God

My Plan Today:

Transformation

- Interactive reading and prayer of one chapter from Psalms or Proverbs

My Plan Today:

Communication

- Prayer for personal needs
- Prayer for needs of others
- Prayer of casting cares upon the Lord
- Prayer of claiming a promise from God

My Plan Today:

Devotional Journal

Meditation

What did God show me about Himself?

What verse or truth from my two Bible readings will I meditate on day and night?

Application

What did God, through His Word, tell me to do?

Other Thoughts

Devotional Planner

Date: ____________________

Preparation

Prayer ◆ Song ◆ Reading of a Christian book

My Plan Today:

Confession

- Confession of known sin

My Plan Today:

Search Me, O God

Revelation

- Reading to know God through one Bible passage

My Plan Today:

Adoration

- Prayer and songs of praise
- Prayer and songs of thanksgiving
- Praying the names of God

My Plan Today:

Transformation

- Interactive reading and prayer of one chapter from Psalms or Proverbs

My Plan Today:

Communication

- Prayer for personal needs
- Prayer for needs of others
- Prayer of casting cares upon the Lord
- Prayer of claiming a promise from God

My Plan Today:

Devotional Journal

Meditation

What did God show me about Himself?

What verse or truth from my two Bible readings will I meditate on day and night?

Application

What did God, through His Word, tell me to do?

Other Thoughts

Devotional Planner

Date: ____________________

Preparation

Prayer ◆ Song ◆ Reading of a Christian book

My Plan Today:

Confession

- Confession of known sin

My Plan Today:

Search Me, O God

Revelation

- Reading to know God through one Bible passage

My Plan Today:

Adoration

- Prayer and songs of praise
- Prayer and songs of thanksgiving
- Praying the names of God

My Plan Today:

Transformation

- Interactive reading and prayer of one chapter from Psalms or Proverbs

My Plan Today:

Communication

- Prayer for personal needs
- Prayer for needs of others
- Prayer of casting cares upon the Lord
- Prayer of claiming a promise from God

My Plan Today:

Devotional Journal

Meditation

What did God show me about Himself?

What verse or truth from my two Bible readings will I meditate on day and night?

Application

What did God, through His Word, tell me to do?

Other Thoughts

Devotional Planner

Date: ____________________

Preparation

Prayer ◆ Song ◆ Reading of a Christian book

My Plan Today:

Confession

- Confession of known sin

My Plan Today:

Search Me, O God

Revelation

- Reading to know God through one Bible passage

My Plan Today:

Adoration

- Prayer and songs of praise
- Prayer and songs of thanksgiving
- Praying the names of God

My Plan Today:

Transformation

- Interactive reading and prayer of one chapter from Psalms or Proverbs

My Plan Today:

Communication

- Prayer for personal needs
- Prayer for needs of others
- Prayer of casting cares upon the Lord
- Prayer of claiming a promise from God

My Plan Today:

Devotional Journal

Meditation

What did God show me about Himself?

What verse or truth from my two Bible readings will I meditate on day and night?

Application

What did God, through His Word, tell me to do?

Other Thoughts

Devotional Planner

Date: ____________________

Preparation

Prayer ◆ Song ◆ Reading of a Christian book

My Plan Today:

Confession

- Confession of known sin

My Plan Today:

Search Me, O God

Revelation

- Reading to know God through one Bible passage

My Plan Today:

Adoration

- Prayer and songs of praise
- Prayer and songs of thanksgiving
- Praying the names of God

My Plan Today:

Transformation

- Interactive reading and prayer of one chapter from Psalms or Proverbs

My Plan Today:

Communication

- Prayer for personal needs
- Prayer for needs of others
- Prayer of casting cares upon the Lord
- Prayer of claiming a promise from God

My Plan Today:

Devotional Journal

Meditation

What did God show me about Himself?

What verse or truth from my two Bible readings will I meditate on day and night?

Application

What did God, through His Word, tell me to do?

Other Thoughts

Devotional Planner

Date: ____________________

Preparation

Prayer ◆ Song ◆ Reading of a Christian book

My Plan Today:

Confession

- Confession of known sin

My Plan Today:

Search Me, O God

Revelation

- Reading to know God through one Bible passage

My Plan Today:

Adoration

- Prayer and songs of praise
- Prayer and songs of thanksgiving
- Praying the names of God

My Plan Today:

Transformation

- Interactive reading and prayer of one chapter from Psalms or Proverbs

My Plan Today:

Communication

- Prayer for personal needs
- Prayer for needs of others
- Prayer of casting cares upon the Lord
- Prayer of claiming a promise from God

My Plan Today:

Devotional Journal

Meditation

What did God show me about Himself?

What verse or truth from my two Bible readings will I meditate on day and night?

Application

What did God, through His Word, tell me to do?

Other Thoughts

Devotional Planner

Date: ______________

Preparation

Prayer ◆ Song ◆ Reading of a Christian book

My Plan Today:

Confession

- Confession of known sin

My Plan Today:

Search Me, O God

Revelation

- Reading to know God through one Bible passage

My Plan Today:

Adoration

- Prayer and songs of praise
- Prayer and songs of thanksgiving
- Praying the names of God

My Plan Today:

Transformation

- Interactive reading and prayer of one chapter from Psalms or Proverbs

My Plan Today:

Communication

- Prayer for personal needs
- Prayer for needs of others
- Prayer of casting cares upon the Lord
- Prayer of claiming a promise from God

My Plan Today:

Devotional Journal

Meditation

What did God show me about Himself?

What verse or truth from my two Bible readings will I meditate on day and night?

Application

What did God, through His Word, tell me to do?

Other Thoughts

Devotional Planner

Date: ___________________

Preparation

Prayer ◆ Song ◆ Reading of a Christian book

My Plan Today:

Confession

- Confession of known sin

My Plan Today:

Search Me, O God

Revelation

- Reading to know God through one Bible passage

My Plan Today:

Adoration

- Prayer and songs of praise
- Prayer and songs of thanksgiving
- Praying the names of God

My Plan Today:

Transformation

- Interactive reading and prayer of one chapter from Psalms or Proverbs

My Plan Today:

Communication

- Prayer for personal needs
- Prayer for needs of others
- Prayer of casting cares upon the Lord
- Prayer of claiming a promise from God

My Plan Today:

Devotional Journal

Meditation

What did God show me about Himself?

What verse or truth from my two Bible readings will I meditate on day and night?

Application

What did God, through His Word, tell me to do?

Other Thoughts

Devotional Planner

Date: ____________________

Preparation

Prayer ◆ Song ◆ Reading of a Christian book

My Plan Today:

Confession

- Confession of known sin

My Plan Today:

Search Me, O God

Revelation

- Reading to know God through one Bible passage

My Plan Today:

Adoration

- Prayer and songs of praise
- Prayer and songs of thanksgiving
- Praying the names of God

My Plan Today:

Transformation

- Interactive reading and prayer of one chapter from Psalms or Proverbs

My Plan Today:

Communication

- Prayer for personal needs
- Prayer for needs of others
- Prayer of casting cares upon the Lord
- Prayer of claiming a promise from God

My Plan Today:

Devotional Journal

Meditation

What did God show me about Himself?

What verse or truth from my two Bible readings will I meditate on day and night?

Application

What did God, through His Word, tell me to do?

Other Thoughts

Devotional Planner

Date: ____________

Preparation

Prayer ◆ Song ◆ Reading of a Christian book

My Plan Today:

Confession

- Confession of known sin

My Plan Today:

Search Me, O God

Revelation

- Reading to know God through one Bible passage

My Plan Today:

Adoration

- Prayer and songs of praise
- Prayer and songs of thanksgiving
- Praying the names of God

My Plan Today:

Transformation

- Interactive reading and prayer of one chapter from Psalms or Proverbs

My Plan Today:

Communication

- Prayer for personal needs
- Prayer for needs of others
- Prayer of casting cares upon the Lord
- Prayer of claiming a promise from God

My Plan Today:

Devotional Journal

Meditation

What did God show me about Himself?

What verse or truth from my two Bible readings will I meditate on day and night?

Application

What did God, through His Word, tell me to do?

Other Thoughts

Devotional Planner

Date: ____________________

Preparation

Prayer ◆ Song ◆ Reading of a Christian book

My Plan Today:

Confession

- Confession of known sin

My Plan Today:

Search Me, O God

Revelation

- Reading to know God through one Bible passage

My Plan Today:

Adoration

- Prayer and songs of praise
- Prayer and songs of thanksgiving
- Praying the names of God

My Plan Today:

Transformation

- Interactive reading and prayer of one chapter from Psalms or Proverbs

My Plan Today:

Communication

- Prayer for personal needs
- Prayer for needs of others
- Prayer of casting cares upon the Lord
- Prayer of claiming a promise from God

My Plan Today:

Devotional Journal

Meditation

What did God show me about Himself?

What verse or truth from my two Bible readings will I meditate on day and night?

Application

What did God, through His Word, tell me to do?

Other Thoughts

Devotional Planner

Date: ________________

Preparation

Prayer ◆ Song ◆ Reading of a Christian book

My Plan Today:

Confession

- Confession of known sin

My Plan Today:

Search Me, O God

Revelation

- Reading to know God through one Bible passage

My Plan Today:

Adoration

- Prayer and songs of praise
- Prayer and songs of thanksgiving
- Praying the names of God

My Plan Today:

Transformation

- Interactive reading and prayer of one chapter from Psalms or Proverbs

My Plan Today:

Communication

- Prayer for personal needs
- Prayer for needs of others
- Prayer of casting cares upon the Lord
- Prayer of claiming a promise from God

My Plan Today:

Devotional Journal

Meditation

What did God show me about Himself?

What verse or truth from my two Bible readings will I meditate on day and night?

Application

What did God, through His Word, tell me to do?

Other Thoughts

Devotional Planner

Date: ______________

Preparation

Prayer ◆ Song ◆ Reading of a Christian book

My Plan Today:

Confession

- Confession of known sin

My Plan Today:

Search Me, O God

Revelation

- Reading to know God through one Bible passage

My Plan Today:

Adoration

- Prayer and songs of praise
- Prayer and songs of thanksgiving
- Praying the names of God

My Plan Today:

Transformation

- Interactive reading and prayer of one chapter from Psalms or Proverbs

My Plan Today:

Communication

- Prayer for personal needs
- Prayer for needs of others
- Prayer of casting cares upon the Lord
- Prayer of claiming a promise from God

My Plan Today:

Devotional Journal

Meditation

What did God show me about Himself?

What verse or truth from my two Bible readings will I meditate on day and night?

Application

What did God, through His Word, tell me to do?

Other Thoughts

Devotional Planner

Date: ____________

Preparation

Prayer ◆ Song ◆ Reading of a Christian book

My Plan Today:

Confession

- Confession of known sin

My Plan Today:

Search Me, O God

Revelation

- Reading to know God through one Bible passage

My Plan Today:

Adoration

- Prayer and songs of praise
- Prayer and songs of thanksgiving
- Praying the names of God

My Plan Today:

Transformation

- Interactive reading and prayer of one chapter from Psalms or Proverbs

My Plan Today:

Communication

- Prayer for personal needs
- Prayer for needs of others
- Prayer of casting cares upon the Lord
- Prayer of claiming a promise from God

My Plan Today:

Devotional Journal

Meditation

What did God show me about Himself?

What verse or truth from my two Bible readings will I meditate on day and night?

Application

What did God, through His Word, tell me to do?

Other Thoughts

Devotional Planner

Date: ____________________

Preparation

Prayer ◆ Song ◆ Reading of a Christian book

My Plan Today:

Confession

- Confession of known sin

My Plan Today:

Search Me, O God

Revelation

- Reading to know God through one Bible passage

My Plan Today:

Adoration

- Prayer and songs of praise
- Prayer and songs of thanksgiving
- Praying the names of God

My Plan Today:

Transformation

- Interactive reading and prayer of one chapter from Psalms or Proverbs

My Plan Today:

Communication

- Prayer for personal needs
- Prayer for needs of others
- Prayer of casting cares upon the Lord
- Prayer of claiming a promise from God

My Plan Today:

Devotional Journal

Meditation

What did God show me about Himself?

What verse or truth from my two Bible readings will I meditate on day and night?

Application

What did God, through His Word, tell me to do?

Other Thoughts

Devotional Planner

Date: ____________________

Preparation

Prayer ◆ Song ◆ Reading of a Christian book

My Plan Today:

Confession

- Confession of known sin

My Plan Today:

Search Me, O God

Revelation

- Reading to know God through one Bible passage

My Plan Today:

Adoration

- Prayer and songs of praise
- Prayer and songs of thanksgiving
- Praying the names of God

My Plan Today:

Transformation

- Interactive reading and prayer of one chapter from Psalms or Proverbs

My Plan Today:

Communication

- Prayer for personal needs
- Prayer for needs of others
- Prayer of casting cares upon the Lord
- Prayer of claiming a promise from God

My Plan Today:

Devotional Journal

Meditation

What did God show me about Himself?

What verse or truth from my two Bible readings will I meditate on day and night?

Application

What did God, through His Word, tell me to do?

Other Thoughts

Devotional Planner

Date: ____________________

Preparation

Prayer ◆ Song ◆ Reading of a Christian book

My Plan Today:

Confession

- Confession of known sin

My Plan Today:

Search Me, O God

Revelation

- Reading to know God through one Bible passage

My Plan Today:

Adoration

- Prayer and songs of praise
- Prayer and songs of thanksgiving
- Praying the names of God

My Plan Today:

Transformation

- Interactive reading and prayer of one chapter from Psalms or Proverbs

My Plan Today:

Communication

- Prayer for personal needs
- Prayer for needs of others
- Prayer of casting cares upon the Lord
- Prayer of claiming a promise from God

My Plan Today:

Devotional Journal

Meditation

What did God show me about Himself?

What verse or truth from my two Bible readings will I meditate on day and night?

Application

What did God, through His Word, tell me to do?

Other Thoughts

Devotional Planner

Date: ____________________

Preparation

Prayer ◆ Song ◆ Reading of a Christian book

My Plan Today:

Confession

- Confession of known sin

My Plan Today:

Search Me, O God

Revelation

- Reading to know God through one Bible passage

My Plan Today:

Adoration

- Prayer and songs of praise
- Prayer and songs of thanksgiving
- Praying the names of God

My Plan Today:

Transformation

- Interactive reading and prayer of one chapter from Psalms or Proverbs

My Plan Today:

Communication

- Prayer for personal needs
- Prayer for needs of others
- Prayer of casting cares upon the Lord
- Prayer of claiming a promise from God

My Plan Today:

Devotional Journal

Meditation

What did God show me about Himself?

What verse or truth from my two Bible readings will I meditate on day and night?

Application

What did God, through His Word, tell me to do?

Other Thoughts

Devotional Planner

Date: ______________

Preparation

Prayer ◆ Song ◆ Reading of a Christian book

My Plan Today:

Confession

- Confession of known sin

My Plan Today:

Search Me, O God

Revelation

- Reading to know God through one Bible passage

My Plan Today:

Adoration

- Prayer and songs of praise
- Prayer and songs of thanksgiving
- Praying the names of God

My Plan Today:

Transformation

- Interactive reading and prayer of one chapter from Psalms or Proverbs

My Plan Today:

Communication

- Prayer for personal needs
- Prayer for needs of others
- Prayer of casting cares upon the Lord
- Prayer of claiming a promise from God

My Plan Today:

Devotional Journal

Meditation

What did God show me about Himself?

What verse or truth from my two Bible readings will I meditate on day and night?

Application

What did God, through His Word, tell me to do?

Other Thoughts

Devotional Planner

Date: ___________________

Preparation

Prayer ◆ Song ◆ Reading of a Christian book

My Plan Today:

Confession

- Confession of known sin

My Plan Today:

Search Me, O God

Revelation

- Reading to know God through one Bible passage

My Plan Today:

Adoration

- Prayer and songs of praise
- Prayer and songs of thanksgiving
- Praying the names of God

My Plan Today:

Transformation

- Interactive reading and prayer of one chapter from Psalms or Proverbs

My Plan Today:

Communication

- Prayer for personal needs
- Prayer for needs of others
- Prayer of casting cares upon the Lord
- Prayer of claiming a promise from God

My Plan Today:

Devotional Journal

Meditation

What did God show me about Himself?

What verse or truth from my two Bible readings will I meditate on day and night?

Application

What did God, through His Word, tell me to do?

Other Thoughts

Devotional Planner

Date: ____________________

Preparation

Prayer ◆ Song ◆ Reading of a Christian book

My Plan Today:

Confession

- Confession of known sin

My Plan Today:

Search Me, O God

Revelation

- Reading to know God through one Bible passage

My Plan Today:

Adoration

- Prayer and songs of praise
- Prayer and songs of thanksgiving
- Praying the names of God

My Plan Today:

Transformation

- Interactive reading and prayer of one chapter from Psalms or Proverbs

My Plan Today:

Communication

- Prayer for personal needs
- Prayer for needs of others
- Prayer of casting cares upon the Lord
- Prayer of claiming a promise from God

My Plan Today:

Devotional Journal

Meditation

What did God show me about Himself?

What verse or truth from my two Bible readings will I meditate on day and night?

Application

What did God, through His Word, tell me to do?

Other Thoughts

Devotional Planner

Date: ____________________

Preparation

Prayer ◆ Song ◆ Reading of a Christian book

My Plan Today:

Confession

- Confession of known sin

My Plan Today:

Search Me, O God

Revelation

- Reading to know God through one Bible passage

My Plan Today:

Adoration

- Prayer and songs of praise
- Prayer and songs of thanksgiving
- Praying the names of God

My Plan Today:

Transformation

- Interactive reading and prayer of one chapter from Psalms or Proverbs

My Plan Today:

Communication

- Prayer for personal needs
- Prayer for needs of others
- Prayer of casting cares upon the Lord
- Prayer of claiming a promise from God

My Plan Today:

Devotional Journal

Meditation

What did God show me about Himself?

What verse or truth from my two Bible readings will I meditate on day and night?

Application

What did God, through His Word, tell me to do?

Other Thoughts

Devotional Planner

Date: ____________________

Preparation

Prayer ◆ Song ◆ Reading of a Christian book

My Plan Today:

Confession

- Confession of known sin

My Plan Today:

Search Me, O God

Revelation

- Reading to know God through one Bible passage

My Plan Today:

Adoration

- Prayer and songs of praise
- Prayer and songs of thanksgiving
- Praying the names of God

My Plan Today:

Transformation

- Interactive reading and prayer of one chapter from Psalms or Proverbs

My Plan Today:

Communication

- Prayer for personal needs
- Prayer for needs of others
- Prayer of casting cares upon the Lord
- Prayer of claiming a promise from God

My Plan Today:

Devotional Journal

Meditation

What did God show me about Himself?

What verse or truth from my two Bible readings will I meditate on day and night?

Application

What did God, through His Word, tell me to do?

Other Thoughts

Devotional Planner

Date: ___________________

Preparation

Prayer ◆ Song ◆ Reading of a Christian book

My Plan Today:

Confession

- Confession of known sin

My Plan Today:

Search Me, O God

Revelation

- Reading to know God through one Bible passage

My Plan Today:

Adoration

- Prayer and songs of praise
- Prayer and songs of thanksgiving
- Praying the names of God

My Plan Today:

Transformation

- Interactive reading and prayer of one chapter from Psalms or Proverbs

My Plan Today:

Communication

- Prayer for personal needs
- Prayer for needs of others
- Prayer of casting cares upon the Lord
- Prayer of claiming a promise from God

My Plan Today:

Devotional Journal

Meditation

What did God show me about Himself?

What verse or truth from my two Bible readings will I meditate on day and night?

Application

What did God, through His Word, tell me to do?

Other Thoughts

Devotional Planner

Date: ____________

Preparation

Prayer ◆ Song ◆ Reading of a Christian book

My Plan Today:

Confession

- Confession of known sin

My Plan Today:

Search Me, O God

Revelation

- Reading to know God through one Bible passage

My Plan Today:

Adoration

- Prayer and songs of praise
- Prayer and songs of thanksgiving
- Praying the names of God

My Plan Today:

Transformation

- Interactive reading and prayer of one chapter from Psalms or Proverbs

My Plan Today:

Communication

- Prayer for personal needs
- Prayer for needs of others
- Prayer of casting cares upon the Lord
- Prayer of claiming a promise from God

My Plan Today:

Devotional Journal

Meditation

What did God show me about Himself?

What verse or truth from my two Bible readings will I meditate on day and night?

Application

What did God, through His Word, tell me to do?

Other Thoughts

My Every-Day Prayer List

Once-a-Week Prayer List

Sunday

Week of : ____________________

Monday

Tuesday

Wednesday

Thursday

Friday
Saturday

My Every-Day Prayer List

Once-a-Week Prayer List

Sunday

Week of : ____________________

Monday

Tuesday

Wednesday
Thursday

Friday
Saturday

My Every-Day Prayer List

Once-a-Week Prayer List

Sunday

Week of : ____________________

Monday

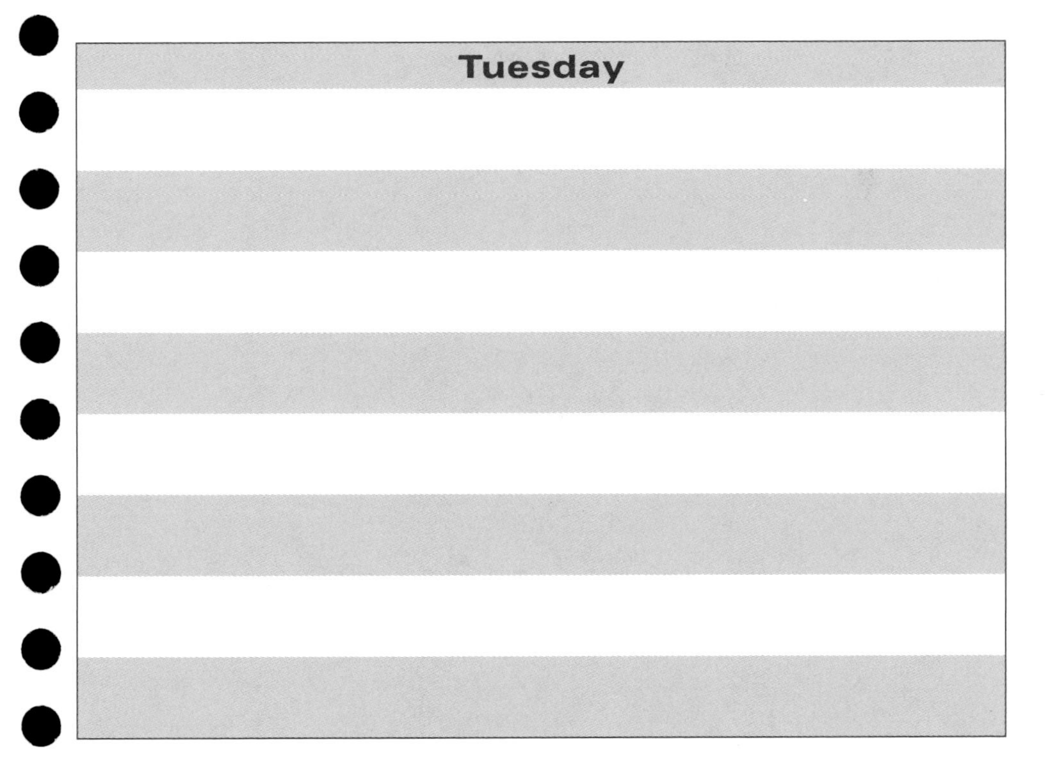

Wednesday

Thursday

Friday
Saturday

My Every-Day Prayer List

Once-a-Week Prayer List

Sunday

Week of : ____________________

Monday

Tuesday

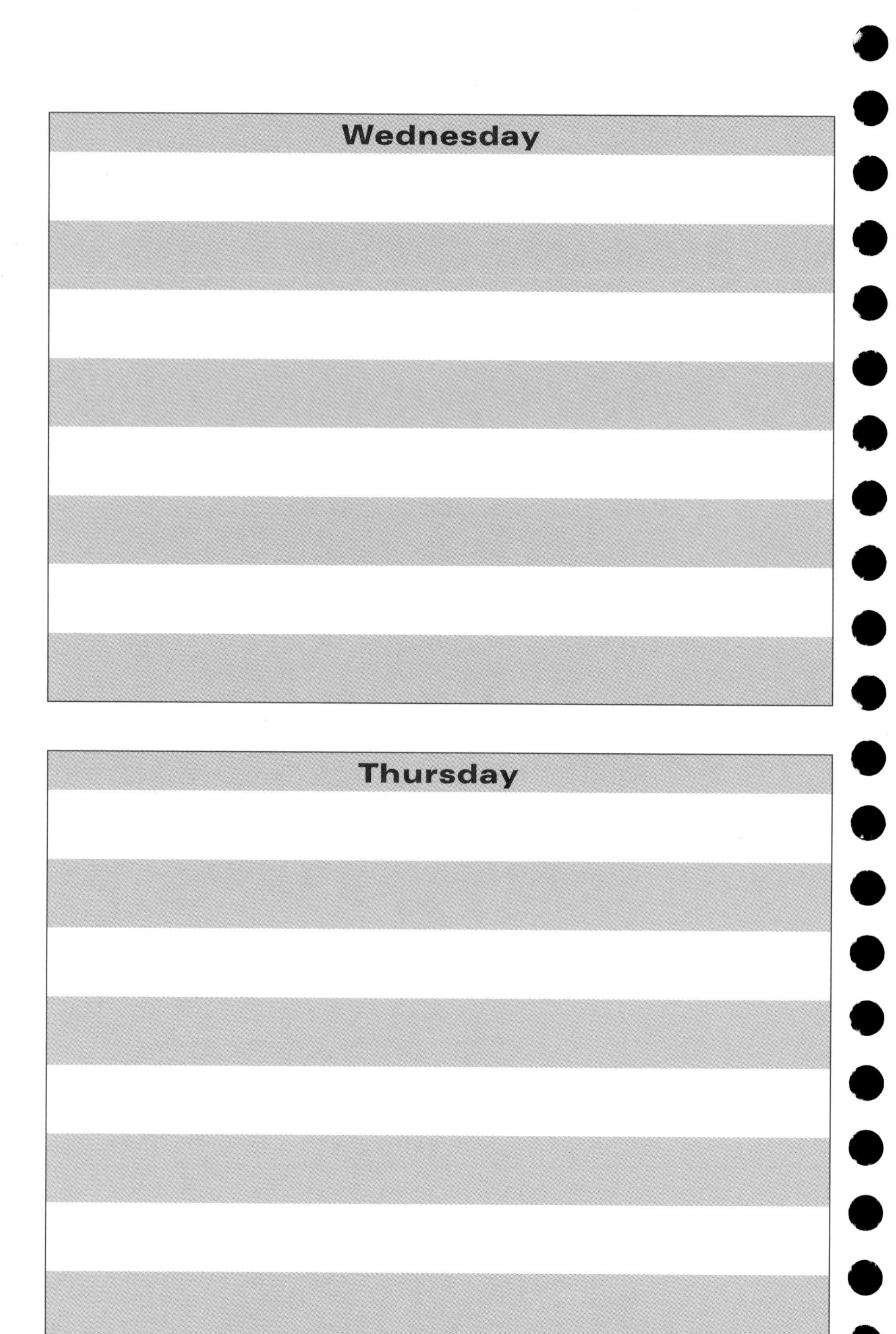
Wednesday
Thursday

Friday
Saturday

My Every-Day Prayer List

Once-a-Week Prayer List

Sunday

Week of : ________________

Monday

Tuesday

Wednesday

Thursday

Friday
Saturday

My Every-Day Prayer List

Once-a-Week Prayer List

Sunday

Week of : ____________________

Monday

Tuesday

Wednesday
Thursday

Friday
Saturday

My Every-Day Prayer List

Once-a-Week Prayer List

Sunday

Week of : ____________________

Monday

Tuesday

Wednesday

Thursday

Friday
Saturday

My Every-Day Prayer List

Once-a-Week Prayer List

Sunday

Week of : ________________

Monday

Tuesday

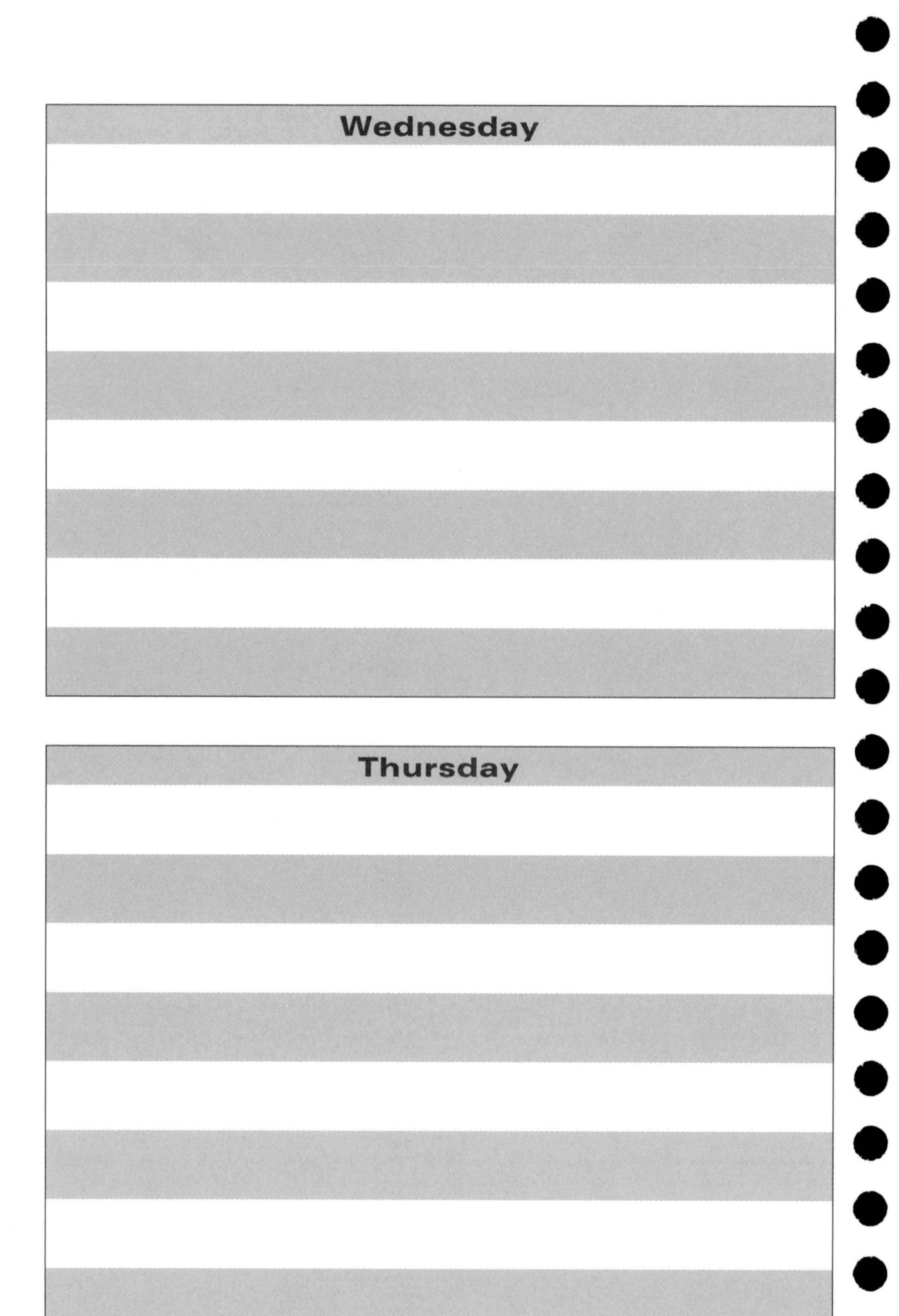
Wednesday
Thursday

Friday
Saturday

My Every-Day Prayer List

Once-a-Week Prayer List

Sunday

Week of : ____________________

Monday

Tuesday

Wednesday

Thursday

Friday
Saturday

My Every-Day Prayer List

Once-a-Week Prayer List

Sunday

Week of : ____________________

Monday

Tuesday

Wednesday

Thursday

Friday

Saturday

My Every-Day Prayer List

Once-a-Week Prayer List

Sunday

Week of : ____________________

Monday

Tuesday

Wednesday

Thursday

Friday

Saturday

My Every-Day Prayer List

Once-a-Week Prayer List

Sunday

Week of : ____________________

Monday

Tuesday

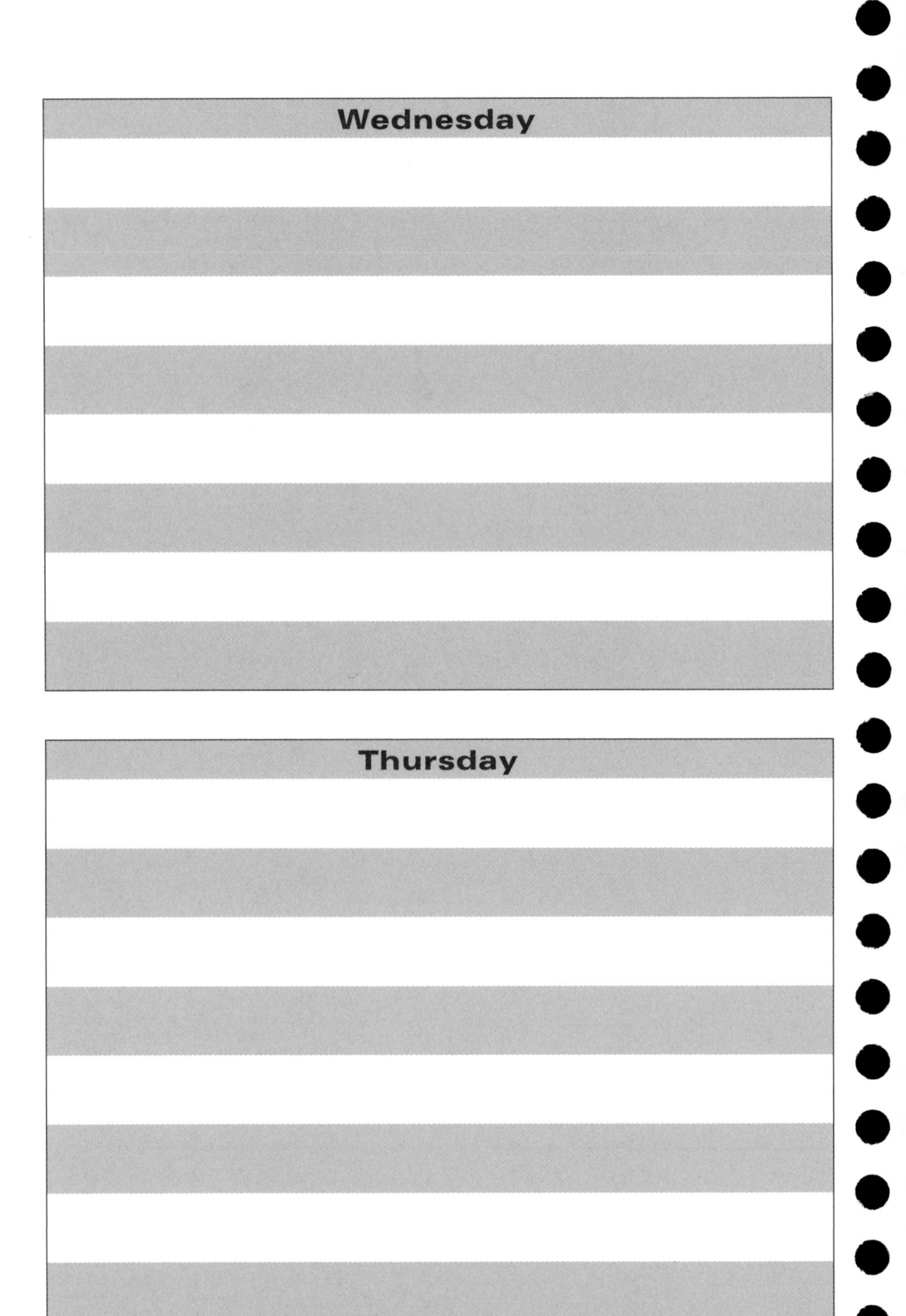
Wednesday
Thursday

Friday
Saturday

My Every-Day Prayer List

Once-a-Week Prayer List

Sunday

Week of : ________________

Monday

Tuesday

Wednesday

Thursday

Friday
Saturday

Song Index

These pages are provided for you to build your own list of songs for your devotions. Most hymnals and songbooks have indexes of songs listed by topic which can be a great help. If you like to use recorded music during your devotions, pull out your music collection and catalog your favorite songs into the appropriate category. The first three categories are directly from the Devotional Planner. I have also added an "Other" category, since you may want to close out your devotional time with a favorite song.

Preparation Songs

Confession Songs

Adoration Songs—Songs of Praise and Thanksgiving

Other Songs

Confession Step Helps

Sins Identified in Scripture

Sins of the Family

1. Adultery
2. Divorce
3. Variance
4. Disobedience to parents
5. Neglect of discipline
6. Dishonor
7. Lack of communication
8. Neglect of family time
9. Neglect of family prayer and devotions
10. Burdensome debt
11. Rebellion in children
12. Husbands not loving their wives
13. Wives not submitting to their husbands
14. Abuse and incest
15. Fighting and bickering
16. Debate and strife
17. Nagging
18. Unwillingness to forgive
19. Complaining
20. Unfaithfulness to church
21. Failure to make reconciliation
22. Failure to witness to your relatives
23. Lack of love

Sins of the Church

1. Failure to pray
2. Whispering/backbiting/ evil speaking
3. Failure to share the gospel
4. False accusations
5. Worldliness
6. Sedition
7. Heresy
8. Laziness of church workers
9. Rebellion against pastoral leadership
10. Failure to be salt in a corrupt world
11. Lukewarmness and carnality
12. Compromise with false doctrine
13. Failure to support missionaries
14. Gossip against church members
15. Powerlessness among believers
16. Neglect of the Holy Spirit's ministry
17. Unbelief of leaders to go forward in faith
18. Immorality of church members
19. Division among believers
20. Participation in wrong music, TV, and movies
21. Lack of love among believers
22. Neglect of attendance to house of worship
23. Failure to respond after hearing the Word

Personal Sins

1. Wickedness/unrighteousness
2. Corrupt communication
3. Reprobate thoughts /lasciviousness/ evil thoughts
4. Maliciousness
5. Pride/headiness/high-mindedness/ boasting
6. Dishonesty/deceit/lying
7. Fornication
8. Murder
9. Witchcraft
10. Lack of mercy/implacableness
11. Strife/reviling
12. Drunkenness
13. Reveling
14. Railing
15. Extortion
16. Blasphemy
17. Foolishness

18. Disorderly conduct/brawling
19. Bitterness
20. Hatred
21. Envy/an evil eye
22. Jealousy
23. Stealing
24. Cursing/Profanity
25. Lust
26. Immorality
27. Idolatry
28. Indulgence
29. Unbelief
30. Lack of self-discipline
31. Unnatural, vile affections/homosexuality
32. Impure thoughts
33. Neglect of the Bible
34. Worldliness
35. Foolish talking/jesting
36. Evil concupiscence
37. Fierceness
38. Covetousness
39. Selfishness
40. Gossip
41. Wrath/anger
42. Greed
43. Criticism
44. Complaining
45. Disrespect
46. Unthankfulness
47. Failure to tithe
48. Laziness
49. Rebellion

Sins of the Nation

1. Abortion
2. Removal of prayer from the public square
3. Homosexuality/unnatural, vile affections
4. Truce/covenant breaking
5. Immorality
6. Loving pleasure more than loving God
7. Materialism
8. Haters of God
9. Menstealers (slavery)
10. Murder
11. Treason
12. Drug abuse
13. Legalized gambling (lottery)
14. Failure to honor the Lord's Day
15. Unbelief in the universities
16. Corruption in government
17. Corruption in entertainment
18. Excessive governmental debt
19. Persecution of Christians

Adapted from *How To Pray Thirty Minutes A Day* by Steve Pettit (used with permission)

Revelation Step Reading Guide

Easy	*Moderate*	*Difficult*
*Genesis	Deuteronomy	Leviticus
Exodus	1 Chronicles	Numbers
Joshua	2 Chronicles	Isaiah
Judges	Job	Jeremiah
Ruth	Song of Solomon	Lamentations
1 Samuel	Romans	Ezekiel
2 Samuel	Galatians	Hosea
1 Kings	Colossians	Joel
2 Kings	Titus	Amos
Ezra	Philemon	Obadiah
Nehemiah	Hebrews	Micah
Esther	Jude	Nahum
Ecclesiastes		Habakkuk
Daniel		Zephaniah
Jonah		Haggai
Matthew		Zechariah
Mark		Malachi
Luke		Revelation
*John		
*Acts		
1 Corinthians		
2 Corinthians		
Ephesians		
Philippians		
1 Thessalonians		
2 Thessalonians		
1 Timothy		
2 Timothy		
*James		
1 Peter		
2 Peter		
*1 John		
2 John		
3 John		

Psalms and Proverbs have been omitted because they are the texts for the Transformation Step.

* The best books to start with if you have never used a Bible reading plan.

Adoration Step Helps

Names of God Identified in Scripture

Names of God the Father

1. A Forgiving God
2. A Fortress of Salvation
3. A Glorious Crown
4. A Jealous and Avenging God
5. A Master in Heaven
6. A Refuge for His People
7. A Refuge for the Poor
8. A Sanctuary
9. A Shade from the Heat
10. A Shelter from the Storm
11. A Source of Strength
12. A Stronghold in Times of Trouble
13. An Ever-present Help in Trouble
14. Architect and Builder
15. Commander of the Lord's Army
16. Creator of Heaven and Earth
17. Defender of Widows
18. Eternal King
19. Father
20. Father of Compassion
21. Father of Our Spirits
22. Father to the fatherless
23. God
24. God Almighty (El Sabbaoth)
25. God Almighty (El Shaddai)
26. God and Father of Our Lord Jesus Christ
27. God Most High
28. God My Maker
29. God My Rock
30. God My Savior
31. God My Stronghold
32. God of Abraham, Isaac, and Jacob
33. God of All Comfort
34. God of Glory
35. God of Gods
36. God of Grace
37. God of Hope
38. God of Love
39. God of Peace
40. God of Retribution
41. God of the Living
42. God of the Spirits of All Mankind
43. God of Truth
44. God Our Father
45. God Our Strength
46. God over All the Kingdoms of the Earth
47. God Who Avenges Me
48. God Who Gives Endurance and Encouragement
49. Great and Awesome God
50. He Who Blots Out Your Transgressions
51. He Who Comforts You
52. He Who Forms the Hearts of All
53. He Who Is Able to Do Immeasurably More Than All We Ask or Imagine
54. He Who Is Able to Keep You From Falling
55. He Who is Ready to Judge the Living and the Dead
56. He Who raised Christ from the Dead
57. He Who Reveals His Thoughts to Man
58. Helper of the Fatherless
59. Holy Father
60. Holy One
61. Holy One Among You
62. I AM
63. I AM WHO I AM
64. Jealous
65. Judge of All the Earth
66. King of Glory
67. King of Heaven
68. Living and True God
69. Lord (Adonai)
70. Lord Almighty
71. Lord God Almighty
72. Lord (Yahweh)
73. Lord Most High

74. Lord My Banner
75. Lord My Rock
76. Lord of All the Earth
77. Lord of Heaven and Earth
78. Lord Our God
79. Lord Our Maker
80. Lord Our Shield
81. Lord Who Heals You
82. Lord Who Is There
83. Lord Who Makes You Holy
84. Lord Will Provide
85. Love
86. Maker of All Things
87. Maker of Heaven and Earth
88. Most High
89. My Advocate
90. My Comforter in sorrow
91. My Confidence
92. My Help
93. My Helper
94. My Hiding Place
95. My Hope
96. My Light
97. My Mighty Rock
98. My Refuge in the Day of Disaster
99. My Refuge In Times of Trouble
100. My Song
101. My Strong Deliverer
102. My Support
103. One to Be Feared
104. Only Wise God
105. Our Dwelling Place
106. Our Judge
107. Our Lawgiver
108. Our Leader
109. Our Mighty One
110. Our Redeemer
111. Our Refuge and Strength
112. Righteous Father
113. Righteous Judge
114. Rock of Our Salvation
115. Shepherd
116. Sovereign Lord
117. The Almighty
118. The Compassionate and Gracious God
119. The Consuming Fire
120. The Eternal God
121. The Everlasting God
122. The Exalted God
123. The Faithful God
124. The Gardener (Husbandman)
125. The Glorious Father
126. The Glory of Israel
127. The God Who Saved Me
128. The God Who Sees Me
129. The Great King Above All Gods
130. The Just and Almighty One
131. The Living Father
132. The Majestic Glory
133. The Majesty of Heaven
134. The One Who Sustains Me
135. The Only God
136. The Potter
137. The Rock in Whom I Take Refuge
138. The Spring of Living Water
139. The Strength of My Heart
140. The True God
141. You Who Hear Prayer
142. You Who Judge Righteously and Test the Heart and Mind
143. You Who Keep Your Covenant of Love with Your Servants
144. You Who Love the People
145. Your Glory
146. Your Praise
147. Your Very Great Reward

Names of Jesus

1. A Banner for the Peoples
2. A Nazarene
3. All
4. Alpha and Omega
5. Ancient of Days
6. Anointed One
7. Apostle and High Priest
8. Author and Perfecter of Our Faith
9. Author of Life
10. Author of Salvation

11. Blessed and Only Ruler
12. Branch of the Lord
13. Bread of God
14. Bread of Life
15. Bridegroom
16. Chief Cornerstone
17. Chief Shepherd
18. Chosen and Precious
19. Cornerstone
20. Christ Jesus My Lord
21. Christ Jesus Our Hope
22. Christ of God
23. Consolation of Israel
24. Covenant of the People
25. Crown of Splendor
26. Eternal Life
27. Faithful and True
28. First to Rise from the Dead
29. Firstborn from Among the Dead
30. Firstborn over All Creation
31. Firstfruits of Those That Have Fallen Asleep
32. Fragrant Offering and Sacrifice to God
33. Friend of Tax Collectors and Sinners
34. God of All the Earth
35. God over All
36. God's Son
37. Great High Priest
38. Great Light
39. Great Shepherd of the Sheep
40. Guarantee of a Better Covenant
41. He Who Comes down from Heaven and Gives Life to the World
42. He Who Died and Came to Life Again
43. He Who Loves Us and Has Freed Us from our Sins
44. He Who Searches Hearts and Minds
45. Head of Every Man
46. Head of the Body (the Church)
47. Head over Every Power and Authority
48. Heir of All Things
49. His One and Only Son
50. Holy and Righteous One
51. Holy One of God
52. Holy Servant Jesus
53. Hope of Israel
54. Horn of Salvation
55. Image of the Invisible God
56. Immanuel (God With Us)
57. Indescribable Gift
58. Jesus
59. Jesus Christ
60. Jesus Christ Our Lord
61. Jesus Christ Our Savior
62. Jesus of Nazareth
63. Judge of the Living and the Dead
64. King Of Kings
65. King of the Ages
66. Lamb of God
67. Light for Revelation to the Gentiles
68. Light of Life
69. Light of Men
70. Light of the World
71. Living Bread That Came Down from Heaven
72. Lord and Savior Jesus Christ
73. Lord (Kurios)
74. Lord Of Lords
75. Lord of Peace
76. Lord of the Harvest
77. Lord of the Sabbath
78. Man Accredited by God
79. Man of Sorrows
80. Master
81. Mediator of a New Covenant
82. Merciful and Faithful High Priest
83. Messenger of the Covenant
84. Messiah
85. Morning Star
86. My Friend
87. My Intercessor
88. One Who Makes Men Holy
89. One Who Speaks to the Father in Our Defense
90. One Who Will Arise to Rule over the Nations

91. Our Glorious Lord Jesus Christ
92. Our Only Sovereign and Lord
93. Our Passover Lamb
94. Our Peace
95. Our Righteousness, Holiness, and Redemption
96. Physician
97. Prince and Savior
98. Prince of Peace
99. Prince of Princes
100. Prince of the Hosts
101. Rabbi/Rabboni (Teacher)
102. Ransom for All Men
103. Refiner and Purifier
104. Resurrection
105. Righteous Judge
106. Righteous Man
107. Righteous One
108. Rock Eternal (Rock of Ages)
109. Ruler of God's Creation
110. Ruler of the Kings of the Earth
111. Savior of the World
112. Second Man
113. Shepherd and Overseer of Your Souls
114. Son of Man
115. Son of the Blessed One
116. Son of the Living One
117. Son of the Most High God
118. Source of Eternal Salvation
119. Sure Foundation
120. Teacher
121. The Amen
122. The Atoning Sacrifice for Our Sins
123. The Beginning and the End
124. The Bright and Morning Star
125. The Exact Representation of His Being
126. The First and the Last
127. The Gate (Door)
128. The Head
129. The Last Adam
130. The Life
131. The Living One
132. The Living Stone
133. The Lord our Righteousness
134. The Man from Heaven
135. The Man Jesus Christ
136. The Most Holy
137. The One and Only
138. The Only God our Savior
139. The Radiance of God's Glory
140. The Rising of the Sun (Dayspring)
141. The Stone the Builders Rejected
142. The Testimony Given in Its Proper Time
143. The True Light
144. The True Vine
145. The Truth
146. The Way
147. The Word (Logos)
148. True Bread from Heaven
149. Wisdom from God
150. Witness to the Peoples
151. Wonderful Counselor
152. Word of God
153. Word of Life
154. Your Life
155. Your Salvation

Names of the Holy Spirit

1. A Deposit (Earnest)
2. Another Counselor
3. Breath of the Almighty
4. Holy One
5. Holy Spirit of God
6. Seal
7. Spirit of Christ
8. Spirit of Counsel and of Power
9. Spirit of Faith
10. Spirit of Fire
11. Spirit of Glory
12. Spirit of God
13. Spirit of Grace and Supplication
14. Spirit of His Son
15. Spirit of Holiness
16. Spirit of Jesus Christ
17. Spirit of Judgement
18. Spirit of Justice

19. Spirit of Knowledge and of the Fear of the Lord
20. Spirit of Life
21. Spirit of our God
22. Spirit of Sonship (Adoption)
23. Spirit of the Living God
24. Spirit of the Lord
25. Spirit of the Sovereign Lord
26. Spirit of Truth
27. Spirit of Wisdom and of Understanding
28. Spirit of Wisdom and Revelation
29. The Gift
30. The Promised Holy Spirit
31. Voice of the Almighty
32. Voice of the Lord

Adapted from *How to Pray Thirty Minutes A Day* by Steve Pettit (used with permission)

Communication Step Bible Promises

100 Favorite Bible Promises by Topic

Number 23:19—God is not man, that He should lie; neither the Son of Man, that He should repent: hath he said, and shall He not do it? or hath He spoken, and shall He not make it good?

2 Peter 1:4—Whereby are given unto us exceeding great and precious promises: that by these ye might be partakers of the divine nature, having escaped the corruption that is in the world through lust.

Anger

Proverbs 15:1—A soft answer turneth away wrath.

Proverbs 25:21–22—If thine enemy be hungry, give him bread to eat; and if he be thirsty, give him water to drink: For thou shalt heap coals of fire upon his head, and the Lord shall reward thee.

Children

Ephesians 6:1–3—Children, obey your parents in the Lord: for this is right. Honour thy father and mother; (which is the first commandment with promise;) That it may be well with thee, and thou mayest live long on the earth.

Comfort

Psalm 46:1–3—God is our refuge and strength, a very present help in trouble. Therefore will not we fear, though the earth be removed, and though the mountains be carried into the midst of the sea; Though the waters therefore roar and be troubled, though the mountains shake with the swelling thereof. Selah.

Psalm 55:22—Cast thy burden upon the Lord, and he shall sustain thee: he shall never suffer the righteous to be moved.

Matthew 11:28—Come unto me, all ye that labour and are heavy laden, and I will give you rest.

Confession and Forgiveness

1 John 1:9—If we confess our sins, he is faithful and just to forgive us our sins, and to cleanse us from all unrighteousness.

Psalm 103:12—As far as the east is from the west, so far hath he removed our transgressions from us.

Jeremiah 31:34—For I will forgive their iniquity, and I will remember their sin no more.

Matthew 6:14—For if ye forgive men their trespasses, your heavenly Father will also forgive you.

Contentment

Hebrews 13:5—Let your conversation be without covetousness; and be content with such things as ye have: for He hath said, I will never leave thee, nor forsake thee.

Correction

Proverbs 3:12—For whom the Lord loveth he correcteth.

Courage

Isaiah 40:29—He giveth power to the faint; and to them that have no might He increaseth strength.

Philippians 4:13—I can do all things through Christ which strengtheneth me.

Death

Psalm 23:4—Yea, though I walk through the valley of the shadow of death, I will fear no evil: for thou art with me; thy rod and thy staff they comfort me.

Enemies

Proverbs 16:7—When a man's ways please the Lord, he maketh even his enemies to be at peace with him.

Hebrew 13:6—So that we may boldly say, The Lord is my helper, and I will not fear what man shall do unto me.

Failure

Psalm 37:23–24—The steps of a good man are ordered by the Lord: and he delighteth in his way. Though he fall, he shall not be utterly cast down: for the Lord upholdeth him with His hand.

Faith

James 1:5–6—If any of you lack wisdom, let him ask of God, that giveth to all men liberally, and upbraideth not; and it shall be given him. But let him ask in faith, nothing wavering. For he that wavereth is like a wave of the sea driven with the wind and tossed.

Faithfulness of God

Psalm 9:10—And they that know thy name will put their trust in thee: for thou, Lord, hast not forsaken them that seek thee.

Fear

Proverbs 1:33—But whoso hearkeneth unto me shall dwell safely, and shall be quiet from fear of evil.

2 Timothy 1:7—For God hath not given us the spirit of fear; but of power, and of love, and of a sound mind.

Proverbs 29:25—The fear of man bringeth a snare: but whoso putteth his trust in the Lord shall be safe.

Freedom from Sin

Romans 6:14—For sin shall not have dominion over you.

Fruitfulness

John 15:5—I am the vine, ye are the branches: he that abideth in me, and I in him, the same bringeth forth much fruit: for without me ye can do nothing.

Giving

Psalm 41:1–2—Blessed is he that considereth the poor: the Lord will deliver him in time of trouble. The Lord will preserve him, and keep him alive; and he shall be blessed upon the earth: and thou wilt not deliver him unto the will of his enemies.

Proverbs 19:17—He that hath pity upon the poor lendeth unto the Lord; and that which he hath given will he pay him again.

Luke 6:38—Give, and it shall be given unto you; good measure, pressed down, and shaken together, and running over, shall men give into your bosom. For with the same measure that ye mete withal it shall be measured to you again.

Proverbs 28:27—He that giveth unto the poor shall not lack: but he that hideth his eyes shall have many a curse.

Growth in Grace

Psalm 138:8—The Lord will perfect that which concerneth me.

Guidance

Proverbs 16:9—A man's heart deviseth his way: but the Lord directeth his steps.

Proverbs 3:5–6—Trust in the Lord with all thine heart; and lean not unto thine own understanding. In all thy ways acknowledge him, and he shall direct thy paths.

John 16:13—Howbeit when he, the Spirit of truth, is come, he will guide you into all truth: for he shall not speak of himself; but whatsoever he shall hear, that shall he speak: and he will shew you things to come.

Help in Trouble

Nahum 1:7—The Lord is good, a strong hold in the day of trouble; and he knoweth them that trust in him.

Psalm 42:11—Why art thou cast down, O my soul? and why art thou disquieted within me? hope thou in God: for I shall yet praise him, who is the health of my countenance, and my God.

Psalm 34:19—Many are the afflictions of the righteous: but the Lord delivereth him out of them all.

Psalm 18:2—The Lord is my rock, and my fortress, and my deliverer; my God, my strength, in whom I will trust; my buckler, and the horn of my salvation, and my high tower.

Honesty

Proverbs 12:19—The lip of truth shall be established for ever: but a lying tongue is but for a moment.

Hospitality

Acts 20:35—It is more blessed to give than to receive.

Humility

Matthew 23:12—And whosoever shall exalt himself shall be abased; and he that shall humble himself shall be exalted.

James 4:6—But he giveth more grace. Wherefore he saith, God resisteth the proud, but giveth grace unto the humble.

Joy

Nehemiah 8:10—For the joy of the Lord is your strength.

Long Life

Proverbs 3:1–2—My son, forget not my law; but let thine heart keep my commandments: For length of days, and long life, and peace, shall they add to thee.

Proverbs 10:27—The fear of the Lord prolongeth days: but the years of the wicked shall be shortened.

Love of God

1 John 4:10—Herein is love, not that we loved God, but that he loved us, and sent his Son to be the propitiation for our sins.

Jeremiah 31:3—The Lord hath appeared of old unto me, saying, Yea, I have loved thee with an everlasting love: therefore with lovingkindness have I drawn thee.

1 John 4:19—We love him, because he first loved us.

Romans 8:38–39—For I am persuaded, that neither death, nor life, nor angels, nor principalities, nor powers, nor things present, nor things to come, Nor height, nor depth, nor any other creature, shall be able to separate us from the love of God, which is in Christ Jesus our Lord.

Loving God

Proverbs 8:17—I love them that love me; and those that seek me early shall find me.

Psalm 37:4—Delight thyself also in the Lord; and he shall give thee the desires of thine heart.

1 Corinthians 2:9—But as it is written, Eye hath not seen, nor ear heard, neither have entered into the heart of man, the things which God hath prepared for them that love him.

Lust

1 John 2:16–17—For all that is in the world, the lust of the flesh, and the lust of the eyes, and the pride of life, is not of the Father, but is of the world. And the world passeth away, and the lust thereof: but he that doeth the will of God abideth for ever.

James 4:7–8—Submit yourselves therefore to God. Resist the devil, and he will flee from you. Draw nigh to God, and He will draw nigh to you.

Meekness

Matthew 5:5—Blessed are the meek: for they shall inherit the earth.

Psalm 22:26—The meek shall eat and be satisfied: they shall praise the Lord that seek Him: your heart shall live for ever.

Mercy

Psalm 103:17—But the mercy of the Lord is from everlasting to everlasting upon them that fear him, and his righteousness unto children's children.

Money

Proverbs 23:5—For riches certainly make themselves wings; they fly away as an eagle toward heaven.

Proverbs 11:28—He that trusteth in his riches shall fall; but the righteous shall flourish as a branch.

Proverbs 28:20—A faithful man shall abound with blessings.

Proverbs 13:7—There is that maketh himself rich, yet hath nothing: there is that maketh himself poor, yet hath great riches.

Obedience

Philippians 4:9—Those things, which ye have both learned, and received, and heard, and seen in me, do: and the God of peace shall be with you.

Romans 8:28—And we know that all things work together for good to them that love God, to them who are the called according to his purpose.

1 John 2:17—And the world passeth away, and the lust thereof: but he that doeth the will of God abideth for ever.

Patience

Galatians 6:9—And let us not be weary in well doing: for in due season we shall reap, if we faint not.

James 1:2–4—My brethren, count it all joy when ye fall into divers temptations; Knowing this, that the trying of your faith worketh patience. But let patience have her perfect work, that ye may be perfect and entire, wanting nothing.

Peace

Philippians 4:7—And the peace of God, which passeth all understanding, shall keep your hearts and minds through Christ Jesus.

John 16:33—These things I have spoken unto you, that in me ye might have peace. In the world ye shall have tribulation: but be of good cheer; I have overcome the world.

Prayer

Matthew 7:7–8—Ask, and it shall be given you; seek, and ye shall find; knock, and it shall be opened unto you; For every one that asketh receiveth; and he that seeketh findeth; and to him that knocketh it shall be opened.

Matthew 21:22—And all things, whatsoever ye shall ask in prayer, believing, ye shall receive.

James 5:16—The effectual fervent prayer of a righteous man availeth much.

Matthew 6:6—But thou, when thou prayest, enter into thy closet, and when thou has shut thy door, pray to thy Father which is in secret; and thy Father which seeth in secret shall reward thee openly.

Pride

Proverbs 16:18—Pride goeth before destruction, and an haughty spirit before a fall.

Mark 9:35—And he sat down, and called the twelve, and saith unto them, If any man desire to be first, the same shall be last of all, and servant of all.

Protection of God

Proverbs 1:33—But whoso hearkeneth unto me shall dwell safely, and shall be quiet from fear of evil.

Psalm 27:1—The Lord is my light and my salvation; whom shall I fear? The Lord is the strength of my life; of whom shall I be afraid?

Righteousness

Psalm 84:11—For the Lord God is a sun and shield: the Lord will give grace and glory: no good thing will he withhold from them that walk uprightly.

Matthew 6:33—But seek ye first the kingdom of God, and his righteousness; and all these things shall be added unto you.

Seeking God

Hebrews 11:6—But without faith it is impossible to please him: for he that cometh to God must believe that he is, and that he is a rewarder of them that diligently seek him.

Lamentations 3:25—The Lord is good unto them that wait for him, to the soul that seeketh him.

Jeremiah 29:13—And ye shall seek me, and find me, when ye shall search for me with all your heart.

Strength

Psalm 73:26—My flesh and my heart faileth: but God is the strength of my heart, and my portion for ever.

Success

Psalm 1:3—And he shall be like a tree planted by the rivers of water, that bringeth forth his fruit in his season; his leaf also shall not whither; and whatsoever he doeth shall prosper.

Joshua 1:8—This book of the law shall not depart out of thy mouth; but thou shalt meditate therein day and night, that thou mayest observe to do according to all that is written therein: for then thou shalt make thy way prosperous, and then thou shalt have good success.

Temptation

1 Corinthians 10:13—There hath no temptation taken you but such as is common to man: but God is faithful, who will not suffer you to be tempted above that ye are able; but will with the temptation also make a way to escape, that ye may be able to bear it.

Hebrews 4:15–16—For we have not an high priest which cannot be touched with the feeling of our infirmities; but was in all points tempted like as we are, yet without sin. Let us therefore come boldly unto the throne of grace, that we may obtain mercy, and find grace to help in time of need.

Trust

Psalm 37:5—Commit thy way unto the Lord; trust also in him; and he shall bring it to pass.

1 Peter 5:7—Casting all your care upon him; for he careth for you.

Waiting on God

Psalm 27:14—Wait on the Lord: be of good courage, and he shall strengthen thine heart: wait, I say, on the Lord.

Wisdom

James 1:5–6—If any of you lack wisdom, let him ask of God, that giveth to all men liberally, and upbraideth not; and it shall be given him. But let him ask in faith, nothing wavering. For he that wavereth is like a wave of the sea driven with the wind and tossed.

Proverbs 28:5—Evil men understand not judgment: but they that seek the Lord understand all things.

Word of God

Romans 1:16—For I am not ashamed of the gospel of Christ: for it is the power of God unto salvation to every one that believeth.

Psalm 119:130 The entrance of thy words giveth light; it giveth understanding unto the simple.

Romans 10:17—So then faith cometh by hearing, and hearing by the word of God.

1 Peter 2:2—As newborn babes, desire the sincere milk of the word, that ye may grow thereby.

Psalm 119:105—Thy word is a lamp unto my feet, and a light unto my path.

Work

Proverbs 28:19—He that tilleth his land shall have plenty of bread: but he that followeth after vain persons shall have poverty enough.

Proverbs 10:4–5—He becometh poor that dealeth with a slack hand: but the hand of the diligent maketh rich. He that gathereth in summer is a wise son: but he that sleepeth in harvest is a son that causeth shame.

Proverbs 20:13—Love not sleep, lest thou come to poverty; open thine eyes, and thou shalt be satisfied with bread.

Worry

Philippians 4:6–7—Be careful for nothing; but in every thing by prayer and supplication with thanksgiving let your requests be made known unto God. And the peace of God, which passeth all understanding, shall keep your hearts and minds through Christ Jesus.

Philippians 4:19—But my God shall supply all your need according to his riches in glory by Christ Jesus.

Alone with **God**

To order extra copies of this journal,
call 1.800.845.5731 or go to
www.bjupress.com